THE BUSH DEVIL ATE SAM...

And Other Tales of A Peace Corps Volunteer in Liberia, West Africa

Curtis Mekemson

To Peggy and her sense of humor.

And to the people of Liberia.

INTRODUCTION

Scruffy soldiers with guns pointed in all directions were scattered around my yard when I returned from teaching. "What's up?" I asked in a shaky voice that was supposed to come out calm. Liberian soldiers were scary.

"Your dog ate one of the Superintendent's guinea fowl," the sergeant growled. The Superintendent was the governor of Bong County. His compound was nearby and he was, apparently, quite fond of his fowl birds. But Boy, the perpetrator of the crime, didn't belong to me, and he regarded my cat Rasputin as dinner.

"Why don't you arrest him," I suggested helpfully.

"Not him. You!" the sergeant roared. "You are coming with us." The interview wasn't going as planned.

"I am not going anywhere with you. He is not my dog," I responded as I disappeared quickly into my house. Yanking a Peace Corps Volunteer out of his home for a dead, want-to-be chicken would have serious repercussions. Or at least I hoped that's what the sergeant would think. He eventually left.

At 4:00 a.m., he was back, pounding on my door with the butt of his rifle.

"Your dog ate another one of the Superintendent's guinea fowl," Sarge announced with glee at the thought of dragging me off into the dark night. I was beginning to seriously question my decision to join the Peace Corps.

Nonetheless, joining was one of the best decisions in my life. The way I was raised and educated, even my DNA, had pointed me in the direction of striking off into the unknown. But there was more. I am very much a 'child of the sixties. Civil Rights, the Vietnam War, and the student revolution dramatically affected how I view the world. Being a student at UC Berkeley during the Free Speech Movement of 1964 provided me with a front-row, head-bashing opportunity for involvement in these issues. Looking back, I can see how the Berkeley experience, my wandering genes, and the influence of family, friends and teachers encouraged me to sign on the dotted line.

In 2007, I was working on a memoir titled "Growing Up in a Graveyard." I had retired from my career as an environmentalist, wilderness guide, and public-health advocate. I needed a new challenge and loved to write. Conventional wisdom and a thousand books on writing dictated I should write about what I knew best. Having finished the first draft, I bravely decided to share the manuscript with the book club my wife Peggy and I had belonged to for 17 years, the Bigger Sacramento Book Club (BSBC). Luckily, the often-feisty members were kind.

At the end of the evening, John Robbins, an iconoclastic professor and physician with the University of California Medical School at Davis, suggested that I pull out the section I had written about my Peace Corps experience and turn it into a book of its own. His suggestion led me to consider the idea. The 50th anniversary of the Peace Corps in 2011 clinched the deal.

John Kennedy created the Peace Corps in 1961 as one of his first acts as President of the United States. His reasons were both idealistic and pragmatic. Yes, he wanted to help third-world countries combat the terrible poverty, disease, hunger, illiteracy and conflict they faced, but he was also interested in winning hearts and minds for the West. Kennedy, like most other leaders of his generation, believed that we were in the midst of a worldwide conflict between capitalism and communism, democracy and totalitarianism, Christianity and Atheism. The Cold War was raging, and much of this war was being fought in third-world countries.

The Peace Corps is one of the most cost-effective foreign-aid programs ever created by the US. It is certainly one of the least expensive— especially when the work Volunteers do overseas and the commitment they bring back home are considered. A 2012 Peace Corps budget justification noted that the total cost of running the Peace Corps for the past 50 years could be covered with what the US spends on the military every five days.

My assignment was to serve as a teacher in Liberia, West Africa. The country has a unique history dating back to the early 19th Century when freed slaves from America were shipped back to Africa. Within 30 years, the freed slaves, or Americo-Liberians as they came to be known, had established themselves as the rulers of Africa's first black republic. When I arrived in 1965, their descendants still controlled the political, military, justice, education and economic systems of Liberia— almost everything. William Shadrach Tubman, President of the country since 1944, had invited Peace Corps into Liberia to help tribal Liberians, 95% of the population, prepare for a larger role in the nation's future. Not all Americo-Liberians agreed with this goal, as I would learn.

The Bush Devil Ate Sam includes a number of stories about the adventures that I, along with my former wife, Jo Ann, had in Africa, but it also contains background on my decision to join the Peace Corps, and some thoughts on the tragic history of Liberia since the 60s. I conclude with a brief overview of the present Ebola crisis. Half of the profits derived from this book will be devoted to helping the people of Liberia combat this frightening epidemic.

So please join me as I leave the chaotic world of UC Berkeley and the student revolution of the mid 60s to become a Peace Corps Volunteer in the even stranger world of Liberia. You will meet fascinating characters like Crazy Flumo, learn valuable new skills such as how to fight off an invasion of army ants, meet a judge who determines guilt with a red-hot machete, and discover why the government determined I was a dangerous revolutionary. And that's only the beginning…

But now, it is time to jump into the book and determine what role DNA played in leading me to leave a small, rural town in Northern California for the far off jungles of West Africa.

CHAPTER 1

BORN TO WANDER

August 1965. Tears tracked across Jo Ann's cheeks. We had just left her parents in San Francisco and boarded a United Airlines jet bound for New York City. We were leaving family, friends and life in the US behind. I was sympathetic with Jo but my mind was elsewhere. While she was grieving over what we had left behind, I was celebrating where we were going. Africa, teaching, and adventure beckoned.

Except for the time when I was 15 and surrendered five hard-earned dollars for a helicopter ride at the El Dorado County Fair, it was my first flight ever. How could I not be excited? The jet taxied out on to the runway, climbed above the Bay, and banked toward the east. For seven hours we would be winging across America and gazing down on cotton clouds, mountain ranges, deserts, rivers, cities, towns, farms and forests.

We waved goodbye to California as the plane flew over the Sierra-Nevada Mountains. The towering granite of the Crystal Range and Pyramid Peak gave way to the deep blue of Lake Tahoe. My mind turned to how the two of us, both from small Northern California towns, had ended up as Peace Corps Volunteers on our way to the remote jungles of West Africa. Certainly the two years we had just spent at UC Berkeley were a factor. Our time at Sierra College near Sacramento had also played an important role, but my reasons went back farther, back to my very beginning.

Family legend is that I was conceived during a moment of weakness when my mother had the flu. For the record, I delivered my first squawk of protest on March 3, 1943 in Ashland, Oregon. At the time, according to Life

Magazine, American and Australian forces were duking it out with the Japanese at the Battle of the Bismarck Sea, bow ties were the hot new fashion with American women, and Westinghouse engineers were firing dead chickens 200 miles per hour at airplane windows. They went splat. Success meant the windows didn't crack.

I grew up in the small town of Diamond Springs, California about 35 miles east of Sacramento. Sleepy is too lively a word for describing the community during the 1940s and 50s. In Old West terminology, Diamond Springs was a one and one half horse town. There was one church, one barbershop, one hardware store, and one grammar school. On the two horse side of the equation, there were two grocery stores, two gas stations, two restaurants, two bars, two graveyards and two major places of employment: the Diamond Lime Company and Caldor, the lumber company where my father, Pop, worked as an electrician.

The town hadn't always been quiet. Located in the foothills of the Sierra Nevada Mountain Range, Diamond Springs was once a major gathering spot for the Maidu Indians, and later became a bustling Gold Rush town. To the Maidu it was Mo-lok'epakan, or, Morning Star's Spring and a very holy place. The Indians came from miles around bearing their dead on litters to burn on pyres. The smoke and spirits were sent wafting through the air to wherever deceased Maidu went. They had lived in the area for a thousand years.

In 1848, John Marshall found some shiny yellow baubles in the American River at Sutter's Mill, 13 miles away. The world of the Maidu and Morning Star's Spring was about to be shattered. "Gold!" went out the cry to Sacramento, across the nation and around the world. Instant wealth was to be had in California and the 49ers were on their way. They came by boat, wagon, horse and foot— whatever it took. And they came in the thousands from Maine to Georgia, Yankee and Southerner alike. They left behind their wives, children, mothers, fathers, and half-plowed fields. The chance of 'striking it rich' was a siren call not to be denied.

Seemingly overnight the once quiet foothills were alive with the sound of the miners' picks and shovels punctuated by the occasional gunshot. Boomtowns sprouted wherever gold was to be found. In 1850 a party of 200 Missourians stopped off at Morning Stars Spring and decided to stay. Timber was plentiful, the grazing good, and a 25-pound nugget of gold was found nearby. Soon there were numerous hotels, stables, a school, churches, doctors, a newspaper, lawyers, vineyards, a blacksmith, some 8000 miners and undoubtedly several unrecorded whorehouses. Morning Stars Spring took on a new name, Diamond Springs. The Wells Fargo Stage Company opened an office and the Pony Express made it a stop on its two-year ride to glory.

By the time the Mekemsons arrived at the end of World War II, Diamond Spring's glory years were over. The gold had long since been mined out, the town had burned down three times, and the population had dropped to somewhere around 700. There wasn't much to do. In this pre-TV era our entertainment depended on our imaginations. For me, this meant disappearing into the woods as soon as I could escape the not too watchful eyes of my parents. While other boys lined up for Little League and batting practice, I was out doing an inventory of the local skunk, coyote and deer population.

I was born to wander; I'm convinced of this. Whatever lies over the next horizon calls to me and pulls me onward. Eventually this need to roam would be a factor in my decision to join the Peace Corps. It may be genetic. I come from a long line of pioneers and adventurers. Before Mother went trolling and landed Pop, he had lived in Nebraska, Washington, Iowa, Oklahoma, Colorado and Oregon. I've no doubt that lacking an anchor of three kids and a wife, he would have kept on going and going, just like the Energizer Bunny. And so it has been with most of my ancestors.

Restless urges sent members of both my mother and father's families on their way to the New World in the 17th and 18th centuries, and kept them moving west in the 19th and 20th. Puritan Marshalls packed their bags and sailed off for the New World in the 1630s. The Scotch-Irish Mekemsons

11

arrived in Pennsylvania from Ireland in the 1750s, spent the Revolutionary War years in upper Maryland, and had moved on to Kentucky by the 1790s. The cry of gold sent both Marshalls and Mekemsons scurrying to California in the 1840s and 50s.

George Marshall left his wife Margaret pregnant with my Great Grandfather on his trip to the goldfields. It was a good thing; no pregnant wife would have meant no Curt. On his way home, Great, Great Grandpa was killed, stripped of his gold, and thrown into the Pacific. It was tough and often deadly on the frontier. Not that this cured any of my family from their wandering ways. The drive to roam far outweighed whatever the risks might be. One of my favorite family stories illustrates just how deadly frontier life could be.

William Brown Mekemson, my great, great uncle, ended up on the wrong end of a tomahawk (or several) during the Black Hawk Indian War of 1832. A 1903 book by Frank Stevens describes the event. The Indians had attacked the night before, stealing a horse. Captain Snyder decided to pursue the Indians the next morning and caught up with them "firmly entrenched in a deep gulch, where, in a sharp hand to hand encounter, all four were killed with the loss of only one man, Private William B. Mekemson, who received two balls in the abdomen, inflicting a mortal wound."

Except it wasn't immediately mortal. Mekemson was placed on a litter and transported back toward camp. Along the way he pleaded for a drink. A squad was assigned to climb down to the creek and fetch water. At that point the Indians struck again. Some 50 or so "hideously yelling, rushed poor Mekemson and chopped off his head with tomahawks…" and then rolled it down the hill. That was mortal.

The greatest wanderer among my modern day relatives was my Grandfather's brother, Edison Marshall, or Uncle Eddie as my mother called him. He was an accomplished writer quite popular in the 20s, 30s, 40s and 50s. His short stories even made it into the high school literature books of the day and nine of his books were converted into movies. The first to obtain silver screen status was "*Strength of the Pines*" in 1922 and the last was "*The Vikings*" starring Kirk Douglas, Tony Curtis, Ernest Borgnine and Janet Leigh in 1958. He had a long and profitable career.

I never met the man; his Augusta, Georgia mansion was a long way from our converted World War II army barracks house in Diamond Springs. But we did have a collection of his autographed books. They were swashbuckling historical novels that had his heroes such as Marco Polo wandering the world. Edison wandered along with them, doing research for the books and pursuing his passion for big game hunting.

We had a hand-me-down 1920's Encyclopedia Britannica atlas of his where he had outlined his personal journeys in the map section. I spent hours staring at ink-drawn lines snaking off into East Africa and other exotic locales trying to imagine his adventures. By 10, I had the reading skills to handle his books but not the maturity, at least according to my parents. His books were restricted for sexual content and I was supposedly banned from reading them until I was thirteen, when I really didn't need anything else to stir up my sexual fantasies.

Uncle Eddie was not noted for humility. "I went after fame and fortune, and I got them both," he reported. That made his lifestyle all the more attractive to me. If he could gain fame and fortune through travel and writing, possibly I could as well. The combination of Edison's books and his atlas gave me an early lust for travel, an appreciation of history, and a desire to someday write.

In 1963 I had my first opportunity to wander away from home. I was accepted as a junior at the University of California in Berkeley, which, at the time, was about to become the center of a worldwide student revolution. My experience at the University, in turn, would lead to an even greater chance to travel: the Peace Corps.

CHAPTER 2

A LEFT TURN FROM THE RIGHT LANE

The first time I voted, I voted for Richard Nixon, I am embarrassed to say; he was running against Jack Kennedy. The decision came naturally— voting Republican was a family tradition. We had Republican roots dating back to Abraham Lincoln. Chester Marshall, Gold Rush George's dad, had been a Baptist preacher and an Illinois abolitionist in the 1850s. He attended conventions and reportedly took part in the Underground Railway. My Great Grandfather, George Jr., claimed in 1920 that every Marshall born since the Civil War had been Republican. George's big issue was immigration. Too many Italians were crossing our borders and staying.

Pop's credentials may have been tainted. He belonged to a union, but he still voted Republican. Abe Lincoln had been a family lawyer to distant cousins and Pop believed that the worst thing that had ever happened to America was Franklin Roosevelt.

So how dedicated was I to the Republican cause? Let me put it this way: my first political debate on behalf of the Grand Old Party put me in the hospital.

I was in the 4th grade and my mom sent me off to school proudly wearing an "I Like Ike" button. It was the 1952 Presidential election and Dwight Eisenhower was running against Adlai Stevenson. Another boy's parents were equally dedicated to Stevenson. The two of us ended up in the boy's restroom in a heated debate and I learned an important political lesson: never argue with someone carrying a baseball bat. Lacking political sophistication, our discussion had quickly deteriorated into name-calling, the heart and soul of most political campaigns. I had a larger vocabulary of four letter words and was winning when the Stevenson devotee wound up and hit me across the thigh with his baseball bat. I ended up in the hospital with a knot on my leg the size of a softball. Like most martyrs, my devotion to the cause was only strengthened.

I graduated from high school Republican to the core and envisioned a future of wealth and power. It was not the type of future that would accommodate a detour to Africa and the Peace Corps.

I was about to make a left turn from the right lane, however. Old values would clash with new. College was looming. I spent my first two years at Sierra: a small, rural community college nestled in the rolling foothills east of Sacramento. I then transferred to the University of California at Berkeley, the flashpoint of worldwide student unrest in the 60s. Sierra would liberalize my view of the world; Berkeley radicalized it.

The process of liberalization started during the first hour on my first day at Sierra. The faculty had arranged for a speaker to kick off the school's Howdy Day welcome. Dr. No Yong Park, a Chinese man with a Harvard education, stood up in front of a sea of white faces and smiled like he had access to secrets we didn't.

"You think I look funny?" our speaker asked with a grin. His question was greeted by nervous laughter. As naive as we were, we still knew enough to be made uncomfortable by such a question.

"Well, I think you look funny," he went on to much more laughter, "and there are a lot more of me who think you look funny than there are of you who think I look funny."

It jolted my perspective. The Civil Rights movement was gaining momentum in the South in the early 60s and I was sympathetic with its objectives. Providing people with equal rights regardless of race, sex, religion or other arbitrary factors seemed like the right thing to do.

But I had never perceived of myself as being a minority. Instead, I belonged to an exclusive club. In 1961 white males dominated the US and the US dominated the world. It was easy to assume that this was how things should be. The fact that it might be otherwise put a new spin on the issue. What if I, or my children, ended up in a situation where we were in the minority and lacked power? I added enlightened self-interest to my list of reasons for supporting human rights.

My second revelation took place when I picked up a book on comparative religion and learned about Mithraism and Zoroastrianism. I caught a glimpse of how much our great monotheistic religions were based on older mythologies. Studying history didn't help. I also learned about inquisitions and holy wars brought about by religious fanaticism. My rock that was Peter made a dramatic shift and relocated itself on an active fault zone. So, I stopped going to church.

Another concept I was introduced to at Sierra was environmental activism. For this, I owe thanks to Danny Langford. Dan liked to talk and could fit more words into a minute than I could in five. One Monday morning he proudly informed me that he had spent his weekend pulling up surveyor stakes in El Dorado Hills, a new development east of Sacramento.

"You did what?" I asked in a shocked and disapproving voice.

"I pulled up stakes to discourage a developer from building houses," he responded in greater detail assuming it would make sense to me. It didn't. Why would someone want to discourage a developer? It seemed positively Anti-American. My Republican roots were offended to the core.

"Why would you pull a destructive stunt like that?" I demanded to know as I thought of a whole day or possibly several days of surveyor work going down the drain.

"It's a beautiful area," Dan responded, "covered with oak trees and grass. They are going to cut down the trees, plant houses, and pave over the grass."

Suddenly what Dan was talking about made sense. I wasn't about to join him on one of his destructive forays, but his comments made me think about how fast we were paving over California. Although I was only 20, many of the places I had wandered so happily as a kid had already met their unhappy demise at the business end of a bulldozer. Progress was how this destruction was defined and progress was a sacred American tradition. For the first time in my life, a question had been inserted into my mind about its value.

The fourth event was one of the most scary our generation would face. All of our lives we had been raised under the threat of a nuclear cloud. We were constantly treated to photographs and television coverage of massive, doomsday explosions and their telltale clouds. In elementary school I had been taught to hide under my desk and cover my face so the exploding glass windows wouldn't blind me.

Atom bombs, which could destroy whole cities and kill millions of people, weren't massive enough. We needed bigger bombs and we needed more. It was important that we could kill everyone in the world several times over and blast ourselves and the rest of life into times that would make the so-called Dark Ages seem like a Sunday picnic in the park.

None of this was our fault, of course. We had the evil, Godless, Russian Communists and their desire to rule the world to blame. Losing a soul to communism was worse than losing a soul to the devil. And maybe it was the same thing. Better Dead than Red was the rallying cry of people whose fingers were very close to the nuclear button.

The closest we have come to the nuclear holocaust took place during two terrifying weeks in late October 1962. I, along with most of the student body and faculty at Sierra College, sat tethered to the radio in the Campus Center as our nation teetered on the edge of nuclear abyss. It had all come about because a cigar chomping left-wing dictator we didn't like had replaced a cigar chomping right-wing dictator we did. It was known as the

Cuban Missile Crisis, and has its own headlines in the history books as being a highlight of the Cold War.

Castro and his revolution had provided a toehold for Communism in the western Hemisphere. Jack Kennedy had waged a crusade to get rid of him that had started with alleged assassination attempts using Mafia hit men and ended in the fiasco known as the Bay of Pigs. Castro had then called on Uncle Khrushchev to loan him something to make the USA behave. Russia had responded by offering nuclear missiles.

The thought of having nuclear missiles pointed down the throat of our Eastern seaboard made the folks in Washington rightfully nervous, so Kennedy set up a blockade of Cuba. Fortunately, aided by promises that the US wouldn't invade Cuba and that we would remove our missiles from Turkey, Khrushchev blinked. From that point on in my life, I became convinced that there had to be solutions to solving international differences beyond blowing each other off the map. Nation states rattling sabers was one thing; rattling nuclear bombs was something else.

So here I was in mid-1963, a budding peacenik with international leanings, something of an agnostic, environmentally concerned, and committed to Civil Rights. I had definitely become more liberal in my perspective. I figured I was ready for Berkeley. Not. But I was approaching the point where deciding to join the Peace Corps would be natural.

CHAPTER 3

HELD AT GUNPOINT—
TRAINING FOR BERKELEY,
AND THE PEACE CORPS

The man leaned on the front of my 56 Chevy and rested his rifle on the hood. The message was clear. I wasn't going anywhere. Ten minutes earlier I had been happily sleeping in my trailer next to the Lake Tahoe laundry where I was working for the summer. I woke up and jumped out of bed at the sound of trucks warming up. Oversleeping was no excuse for being late. I looked accusingly at my alarm clock. It said 6 a.m. Glancing out the window, I spotted an armed man standing in front of my door. Several others were wandering around the property. The laundry truck drivers were people I didn't recognize. Lacking a phone to call my boss, I decided it was time to vacate the premises.

The summer between my freshman and sophomore year at Sierra College I had graduated from working on pear ranches to being a laundryman. Every afternoon at one o'clock I would zip over to Placerville, pick up clean laundry and head over the mountains to Lake Tahoe via Echo Summit on Highway 50. It was a great job for a college kid. I was provided with a new VW van and was totally on my own except for loading up in Placerville and making my stops at the Lake. In between was a beautiful drive through the Sierra Nevada Mountains. There was even a touch of glamour to the work.

One of my daily stops at the Lake was Bill Harrah's home. He was incredibly rich from his gambling empire, and his home seemed palatial to me. Never having mastered the servant concept, I always made my deliveries to the front door and was occasionally greeted by his headline performers who stayed there. This came to a screeching halt one day when Liza Minnelli opened the door in her baby doll pajamas. She didn't seem to mind my admiration, but the major domo directed me to make all future deliveries to the service entry in the back. I had little appreciation for my new backdoor status.

The best aspect of the laundry business was that the pay was four times what I had earned working in fruit orchards. Since I lived at home, I was able to stash most of my income away for college needs. Eventually, this would pay the majority of my expenses at Berkeley.

The summer of 1963 marked the break between my college years at Sierra and Berkeley. Roger Douvers, the owner of the laundry business, asked if I would like to move up to Lake Tahoe and work for his son-in-law, John Cefalu. John had taken over a laundry that Douvers had owned, sold, and then reclaimed because of back payments. There was an old trailer sitting next to the laundry 'in need of a little work' that I would be welcome to use. I jumped at the chance. What twenty-year-old male given a chance to work in one of the world's top resort areas wouldn't? The only disadvantage, from my perspective, was the distance from my girlfriend. At least, I consoled myself, there was a beach three blocks away that was normally filled with scantily clad young women. I'd get by.

Things, of course, are rarely as rosy as they seem. To start with, the trailer was a mess. It was probably twenty years old and, as far as I could tell, no one had cleaned it in nineteen. My first weekend was devoted to twenty hours of scrubbing. There were no scantily clad women for Curt. Monday brought work, and it was work. I no longer had my leisurely trip back and forth across the mountains. It was stuff the truck with a mountain of clean linen, dash out to the motels and make deliveries, cram the truck up with dirty linen, and rush back to the laundry— over and over and over. I was reminded of the red ants at home and their ceaseless round of chores: go out, get food, bring it back and go out again.

Fatigue, by the end of the day, usually meant I would crawl in bed and go to sleep. A romantic lifestyle it was not. The second weekend, I made an obligatory trip to the beach for Female Body Appreciation 101. But I had no desire for any other relationship and most of what my excursion did was to remind me of what I was missing. I did say mostly, didn't I? The age of the 'itsy bitsy, teeny weenie, yellow polka dot bikini' was dawning, and it was a sight to inspire bad poetry. Not even true love can totally deaden 20-year-old hormones.

My humdrum, ant-like existence came to an end the morning I heard the roar of laundry trucks. I threw on my clothes, sidestepped the gunman guarding my door and jumped into my car. The guard immediately repositioned himself as a hood ornament and looked threatening. Guys with guns can do that.

"Don't be worried, Curt," a familiar voice told me.

"Right," I thought as I checked out the tough looking goon. I turned my head and spotted Woody, our lead driver. "What in the hell is going on?" I demanded.

"We've taken over the laundry," Woody replied casually.

The next question followed naturally: who in the hell constituted we? Woody had an answer for that, too.

"I work for the people that Douvers screwed when he took the laundry back," he told me. "We're here legally. These armed men are professional security guards we hired to protect our interests." Apparently Woody had been quietly arranging a coup while taking Roger's money.

"I am leaving now," I informed Woody.

"I don't think so," Woody replied. "Relax, it will all be over in a few hours and you can go to work for us."

I was beginning to feel like I had been caught up in a Grade B movie.

"Woody, you are not going to shoot me," I said with a lot more confidence than I felt. "Tell the man to get out of my way." I was irritated to the point of irrationality. I turned on the car and started rolling forward. At the last possible moment, when it was clear that I intended to keep going, Woody motioned for his man to move. I was glad they couldn't hear my sigh of relief over the sound of the engine.

Once away from the laundry, I shoved the gas pedal down and made a dash for Cefalu's house. I knocked on the door of the dark house and was surprised to find Roger open it in his pajamas. He'd come up the night before.

"What's wrong Curt," he said sounding a little alarmed. Obviously I wouldn't show up at 6:30 a.m. to wish him a good morning.

"Your laundry has been taken over by armed men," I blurted out and then quickly filled in the details. Roger responded by saying some very unpleasant things. He grabbed his jacket, yelled for his daughter to call the sheriff and told me to jump in his truck. There are three red lights between where Cefalu lived and the laundry. We ran all three. Our truck screeched to a halt in front of the office and Roger jumped out with me close behind.

Fine, I thought to myself. I just escaped from this place and here I am back providing muscle back up for an angry man who is probably going to pop someone in the nose and get us both shot. Fortunately there were a lot of words before any action, and the Sheriff's deputy showed up with siren blasting. It would all be settled in court. I was still in one piece and my experience at facing armed men would make a good story. I had no clue at the time that it would also help prepare me for facing men with guns as a student at Berkeley and as a Peace Corps Volunteer in Africa.

CHAPTER 4

NOVEMBER 23, 1963— THE DEATH OF DREAMS

Berkeley existed in a different world, or possibly, I should say worlds. There was the University and the community surrounding it.

Telegraph Avenue became my mecca. Exotic smells emanated from a dozen different ethnic restaurants, while numerous languages assaulted my ears. I quickly discovered the Café Mediterraneum. In an era before Starbucks made coffee houses safe for middleclass America, Café Med was an original. It was a microcosm of Berkeley, filled with offbeat characters, esoteric discussions and great coffee. I became addicted to both the cappuccino and atmosphere. I would grab my coffee and climb the narrow wooden stairs in back for a coveted balcony seat where I would watch the ebb and flow of the city's unique flotsam.

A quick jaunt across Telegraph produced another treasure, Cody's bookstore. Started on a shoestring by the Cody family in the 50s, it had become one of America's premier bookstores by the mid-sixties. I saved my explorations for Saturdays when there was time to indulge my passion for books. I would disappear inside and become lost to everything except the next title.

I was equally fascinated by the ever-changing kaleidoscope of soapbox oratory provided at the south entrance to the campus on the corner of Bancroft and Telegraph. During any given hour, a dozen speakers could be found there espousing as many causes. I considered it high entertainment and would sit on the steps of the Student Union and listen during breaks from my studies. Over one lunch period, I reported in a letter home, I listened to a student who had spent her summer working in the South registering voters, a black South African talking about apartheid, a socialist railing against the evils of capitalism, a capitalist railing against the evils of social-ism and a Bible thumper detailing out the many paths Berkeley students were following to hell. Apparently, there were too many to count.

Many of the speakers urged that there was more to college life than stud-ies, football and parties. Change was in the wind and we should be part of it. Work for fair housing in Berkeley; oppose the unfair hiring practices at Safeway; sign up to help on a political campaign. Join CORE, SNCC, SLATE, SDS, YAF or a world of other acronyms. I struggled to take it all in, absorb it through my pores. It certainly wasn't Kansas, Dorothy, nor was it Diamond Springs, Placerville or Sierra College.

To simplify my first year I opted to live in a college dorm. I would have a room, a bed and regular meals. The University assigned me to Priestly Hall, which was ideally located a block away from campus and a block away from Telegraph Avenue. Three other dorms, one for men and two for women, comprised our corner of the universe. Co-ed living accommoda-tions were still in the future. Strict House Mothers existed to enforce the rules and protect their charges. Women were only allowed on the first floor of the men's residence hall. Slipping one up to your room was an expellable offense.

Each dorm was nine stories high, brand-new and exactly the same as the others. One of the grad students responsible for our well being immedi-ately dubbed them monstrosities of oblivion. My sixth floor room came complete with a roommate, Clifford Marks. Cliff was a slightly built young man with bright red hair, freckles and a mischievous personality. Later we would share an apartment together. Like me, he was a political science major. Eventually, he too would join the Peace Corps.

As for life at Berkeley, I wanted it all. There were student politics to jump into, classes to master, a love life to support, bookstores to explore, cappuccino to consume and a thousand causes to sort out. Moderation was not an option.

I did understand that my primary reason for being there was to learn and I soon discovered that learning was defined differently than at Sierra. First I had to find my classes. Berkeley seemed like a maze to me. Single buildings held more classrooms than were found on Sierra's campus, and each building held its own secrets. The Life Science building, for example, displayed enough jars of pickled fetuses to stop the heart of a pro-lifer and give me nightmares.

While the Social Science buildings weren't nearly as interesting, I was searching for a political science class in Wheeler Hall when I came upon a string of marble encased urinals in the basement capable of accommodating the whole beer soaked population of an Oakland Raiders football game. I decided there was enough marble to refurbish the Parthenon, which led my mind to contemplate penning a new poem, 'Ode to a Grecian Urinal.' Stream of conscious thinking can be dangerous.

I finally found the class and discovered I had over 1000 classmates. It was located in a large auditorium I had passed by because my mind hadn't been able to comprehend a classroom of that size. The professor, Peter Odegard, was a star in the field of political science and frequently received standing ovations for his stirring lectures. In another life, he had served as President of Reed College in Oregon. His lectures inspired me but there was scant chance I would ever meet the man. Personal contact was through graduate teaching assistants, folks struggling to complete their own education while being paid minimum wages to interact with us. I had one class that was so large we had to sit in another classroom and watch the professor on television. This was mass education on a grand scale and the University's job, according to Clark Kerr, the University President, was the mass production of educated people to go out and fill slots in society.

It was easy to be overwhelmed. I was assigned 15 books in one class and actually thought I was expected to buy and read each one in detail. I was a fast reader but not that fast, nor that wealthy. It would take a year to master the art of skimming, buying old books, using commercially prepared notes and pursuing all of the other tricks of the trade that getting a higher education entailed.

For all of that, there was an excitement to the classes that was lacking at Sierra. I might be sharing my professor with a thousand other students, but he or she might also be a confidante of Presidents. Did I learn more than I had at Sierra? I actually don't think so, but I did have a sense of being part of what was happening in the world and this made what I was learning seem more relevant.

Life quickly evolved into a routine that primarily consisted of attending classes and studying. Mainly I lived in the Bancroft library with occasional forays over to Café Med. Friday nights were reserved for Jo Ann. We had met at Sierra College and fallen in love. We struggled to spend time together, to find moments of privacy and to bridge the gaps that our new life was creating. Even though we had gone off to the University together and now lived less than a mile apart, we saw less of each other than we had at Sierra when we lived 30 miles apart. Dates, given my super tight survival budget, normally consisted in going out for pizza at Laval's or a hamburger at Larry Blake's. Later, when we both turned 21, beer was added to the menu. On rare occasions, we would go to a movie.

Sunday mornings, in lieu of church, I would go for a hike up in the beautiful hills behind Berkeley. There was still solace to be found in the woods.

I had been student body president at Sierra and gamely jumped into student politics at Berkeley. The dormitories were new so the residents were new. They hadn't had time to get to know each other. The fact that I was a community college transfer made little difference. Within a week of my arrival, I was president of Priestly Hall.

Student politics seemed dull and almost frivolous compared to the real thing, though. What truly fascinated me about Berkeley was the palpable sense of being involved in the events of the day. I was drawn toward these issues, and the call to action tweaked my interest. Limiting the future of a potential Martin Luther King, Albert Einstein or Mahatma Gandhi because of whom his parents were went beyond being counterproductive. It was stupid; we all lost. But I wasn't ready to take up a picket sign. This was my first year at Berkeley and my hands were more than full in struggling with classes and eking out time to be with Jo Ann. There were also numerous responsibilities to fulfill in my role as dorm president such as organizing parties and learning Cal football fight songs.

I did strike one tap hammer blow against the machine, however. We were expected to participate in the annual Ugly Man Contest. Its purpose was to raise money for charity by having someone or thing really ugly as the dorm's representative in competition with other dorms, fraternities and sororities. People would vote by donating money (normally pennies) to their favorite ugly man. In addition to being pure fun, it was on the top of the Dean's list as an acceptable student activity.

I proposed that our ugly man be an unfortunate Joe College student whose computer card had been lost by the Administration. Consequently, he no longer existed. Early computers used punched cards to contain data and had become ubiquitous in our lives. They came with the warning "do not fold, spindle or mutilate."

We made up a casket and wandered about campus in search of poor Joe. It was a small thing, but it reflected a growing unease I had about the alienation created by assembly line education where numbers were more important than individuals. It seems that the student body wasn't ready for the message. A popular bartender, selected by a fraternity as its ugly man candidate, walked away with the prize.

While my concerns over student alienation were evolving, the administration was monitoring off-campus student activism with growing concern. The University perceived its primary objectives as carrying out research and preparing young people to become productive members of American society. There was little room in this view for students seeking social and political change— in Mississippi, in Oakland or on campus.

But the world was changing. A young President in Washington was calling on the youth of America to become involved and had created the Peace Corps to encourage involvement. Racial equality seemed attainable in the United States, and people the world over were yearning for and demanding freedom. It was easy for idealistic young Americans to believe we were at the dawning of a new age and natural to want to be involved in the transformation.

Had the students restricted their political efforts in the early and mid sixties to the far off South, the eruption of conflict on the Berkeley Campus may not have taken place. But they chose local targets as well. When the students marched off campus to picket the Oakland Tribune, Sheraton Hotel, United Airways and Safeway over discriminatory hiring practices, they were challenging locally established businesses with considerable power. Not surprisingly, these businesses felt threatened and fought back. Rather than deal with the existing discrimination, they demanded that the University, local authorities, the state government and even the Federal government do whatever was necessary to reign in the protesters.

Their arguments for the crackdown were typical of the times. A few radical off-campus agitators with Communist connections were working in conjunction with left leaning professors to stir up trouble. The participating students lacked mature judgment and were naively being led astray. The vast majority of students were good law abiding kids who just wanted to get an education, party, and get a paycheck.

The University was caught between the proverbial rock and a very hard place. The off-campus political activism was creating unwanted attention. Public dollars could be lost and reputations tarnished. There was a justifiable fear of reprisal from the right. The ugliness of McCarthyism was still alive and well in America. Only a few years before, the House Un-American

Activities Committee (HUAC) had held hearings in San Francisco in its ceaseless search for Commies. UC had been a target.

HUAC created a deep paranoia and distrust within society and may indeed have constituted the most un-American type of activity ever perpetrated on the American public. Clark Kerr and others had worked hard to protect and restore the academic freedom on campus that loyalty oaths and other McCarthy-like activities had threatened. Student activism might refocus right wing attention on the Berkeley Campus.

My greatest insight into the mindset of the Administration was when the Dean of Students called student leaders together to discuss the growing unrest on campus. Our gathering included members of the student government and presidents of the resident halls, fraternities and sororities. Noticeable in their absence were student representatives from off campus organizations such as CORE, SNCC, Young Democrats, Young Republicans and other activist groups. We sat in a large room with tables organized in a square; there must have been at least 40 of us. I was eager to participate and imagined an open discussion of the issues.

The Dean welcomed us, thanked us for agreeing to participate and then laid out the foundation for our discussion. A small group of radical students was disrupting the campus and organizing off-campus activities such as picketing and sit-ins that were illegal in nature. While the issues being addressed were important, there were other, more appropriate means available for solving them that did not involve Berkeley. The Administration had been extremely tolerant so far but was approaching a point where it might have to crack down for the overall good of the University.

The Administration wanted our feedback as student leaders. What did we think was happening, how would our constituencies react to a crack down, and how could we help defuse the situation? We were to go around the room with each student leader expressing his or her view. I expected a major reaction— hopefully a protest or at least a warning to move cautiously, to involve all parties in seeking some type of amenable agreement.

The first student leader stood up. "The radical students are making me extremely angry," he reported. "I resent that a small group of people can ruin everything for the rest of us. The vast majority of the students do not support off-campus political action. I believe the student body would support a crackdown by the Administration. You have my support in whatever you do."

I could not believe what I was hearing. Was the guy a plant, preprogrammed by the Administration to repeat the party line and set the tone for everyone else? If so, he was successful. The next person and the next person parroted what he had said. I began to doubt myself. Normally, I am quite good at reading political trends and sensing when a group leans toward supporting or opposing an issue. My read on what was happening at Bancroft and Telegraph was that the majority of the students were empathic with and supportive of the causes the so-called radical students were advocating.

The Martin Luther Kings of the world were heroes, not bad guys, and their tactics of nonviolent civil disobedience were empowering the powerless. Sure, the majority of the students were primarily concerned with getting through college. To many, an all night kegger and getting laid might seem infinitely more appealing than a sit-in. But this did not imply a lack of shared concern. Or so I believed. Apparently, very few of the other participants shared in my belief. Concerns were raised but no one stopped and said, "Damn it, we have a problem!"

As my turn approached I felt myself chickening out. I was the new kid on the block, wet behind the ears. What did I know? Acceptance in this crowd was to stand up and say, "Yes, everything you are talking about is true. Let's clamp down on the rabble rousers and get on with the important life of being students." And I wanted to be accepted, to be a part of the establishment. I stood up with shaking legs.

"Hi, my name is Curt Mekemson and I am the president of Priestly Hall," I announced in a voice which was matching my legs, shake for shake. This was not the impression I wanted to make. As others had spoken, I had scribbled some notes on what I wanted to say. "I believe we have a very serious problem here, that the issues are legitimate, and that most students are sympathetic. I don't think we should be cracking down but should be working together to find solutions. Now is not the time to further alienate the activists and create more of a crisis than we presently have. I believe it is a serious mistake to not have representatives from the groups involved in organizing off campus activities here today."

I was met with deadly silence. A few heads nodded in agreement, but mainly there were glares. "Next," the Dean said. No yea, no nay, no discussion. I was a bringer of bad tidings, a storm crow. But it wasn't 'kill the messenger.' It was more like 'ignore the messenger,' like I had farted in public and people were embarrassed.

After that, my enthusiasm for student government waned. I should have fought back, fought for what I believed in, fought for what I knew deep down to be right. But I didn't. I was still trying to figure out what to do with 15 books in Poly Sci 1. I had a relationship to maintain on campus and a mother fighting cancer at home. The dark, heavy veil of depression rolled over my mind like the fog rolling in from the Bay. Finally I decided that something had to go and that the only thing expendable was my role as president of the dorm. So I turned over the reins of power to my VP and headed back to Bancroft Library. Politics could wait.

Without student government concerns, Berkeley became more doable and even fun. I disappeared into the library for long hours whipping out term papers, devouring books and becoming a serious student. The end of my first semester approached. Christmas vacation was coming. There would be a break in the endless studies, a time for long walks in the woods and more time for Jo Ann. One crisp fall day in November, I came blinking out of the library to a brilliant sun and a hushed silence. Students and faculty were emptying out of classes; a young woman with long dark hair was standing on the library steps, tears streaming down her face.

"What's wrong?" I asked.

"They've shot the President in Dallas," she replied as her voice broke.

John F. Kennedy was dead. It was November 23, 1963. The young president who was standing up against racism in the South, the man who had created the Peace Corps, who called for international justice and inflamed people's hopes worldwide, had been shot down in the streets of Dallas. And with his death, some of the hope he had created died with him; it died on the Berkeley Campus that day, and it died in me. Each of us lost something of the dream that things could be better, that we as individuals could be better. School stopped and we headed for the nearest TVs, newspapers and radio stations. Time and again we watched the car speeding away with the wounded President, watched Walter Cronkite announce that the President was dead and watched as Lyndon Johnson was sworn in. It was a day etched into the collective memory of our generation.

Thanksgiving arrived and Christmas followed. Somehow I worked up the nerve to ask Jo Ann to marry me. It would be a long engagement with marriage taking place after graduation, a year and a half away. The engagement ring would have to wait for me to dig up the money. She cried and said yes. It was a bright moment of happiness in an otherwise bleak year.

The battle between the Administration and the student activists continued during the spring semester while I focused on studies. On March 3, 1964, I turned 21 and became, according to law, an adult. Soon I would have to decide what I was going to do with my adult life.

CHAPTER 5

ON THE EDGE OF RADICALISM— THE FREE SPEECH MOVEMENT

I came back to Berkeley in the fall of 1964 with a new living arrange-ment. Before summer break, two of my dorm-mates, Cliff Marks and Jerry Silverfield, had agreed to share an apartment with me for our senior year. Landlords had a captive student population to exploit so prices were high. We ended up with a small kitchen, bathroom, living room, and bedroom. Things were so tight in the bedroom that Cliff and I had a bunk bed. He got the top. I would later wonder why this was superior to dorm life. We had more responsibility and less privacy.

We christened the apartment by consuming a small barrel of tequila Cliff had brought back from his summer of sharpening his Spanish skills in Mexico. Later that night, I stood in front of the bathroom mirror and watched myself drool in a hallucinogenic haze, totally fascinated by the process. After going to bed, Cliff talked nonstop. It led me to kick his mat-tress from my lower vantage point. This broke the bed and brought Cliff, mattress and all, tumbling down on me. We were far too gone to put things back together so Cliff ended up sleeping on the floor. We all suffered appro-priately the next day.

While Cliff, Jerry and I were recovering from our well-deserved head-aches, the Administration moved decisively to eliminate on-campus politi-cal activities. There would be no more organizing of community-oriented demonstrations from campus, no more collecting of money from students to support causes, and no more controversial speakers on campus without administrative oversight and control. The Bancroft-Telegraph entrance free speech area was out of business, closed down, caput. That incredible babble of voices advocating a multitude of causes would be heard no more.

The Administration's actions were a testament to the success of the Civil Rights struggle taking place in the Bay Area. It wasn't that the activists wanted change; the problem was that they were achieving it. Non-violent civil disobedience is a powerful tool. Base your fight on moral issues; use the sit-in and the picket line to make your point. When the police come, don't fight back; go limp. If they beat you over the head, you win. Sing songs of peace and justice; put a flower in the barrel of the weapon facing you. It is incredibly hard to fight against these tactics.

As the protests in the surrounding community became more successful, the power structure being attacked struck back. Calls were made to the Regents, the President of the University system, and the Chancellor at Berkeley. 'Control your students or else' was the ominous message. One of the people making the threats was William Knowland, owner of the Oakland Tribune and a former Republican Senator from California who had been a strong supporter of McCarthyism. The Tribune was one of the targets of the anti-discrimination campaign.

The Regents, President and Chancellor bowed to the pressure. Some members of the Administration undoubtedly agreed with Knowland and saw the protesters as part of an anarchic left wing plot. Others may have believed that the students' effectiveness would bring the powers that be down on the university. Academic freedom could be lost. Some likely felt that the activities were disruptive to the education process and out of place on a college campus.

One thing was immediately clear; the Administration woefully underestimated the reaction of the leaders of the various organizations and large segments of the campus population to its dictum. Maybe the administrators actually believed the message they had received from their student leadership the previous fall or maybe they just needed to believe: the out-side pressure was so great it didn't matter how students reacted.

But react they did. These were not young adults whose biggest challenge had been to organize a pre-football game rally. Some, like Mario Savio, had walked the streets of the South and stared racism in the face, risking their lives to do so. That summer while I was driving a laundry truck over the Sierras, three of their colleagues had been shot dead and buried under an earthen dam near Philadelphia, Mississippi. Many had cut their politi-cal eyeteeth four years earlier in the anti House Un-American Activities Committee demonstrations in San Francisco and had participated in the numerous protests against racial discrimination since. They understood the value of demonstrations, media coverage and confrontation, and had become masters at community organization. They were committed to their beliefs and were willing to face police and be arrested if necessary.

The Administration wasn't nearly as focused. Liberal in nature and genu-inely caring for its students, it utilized a 50's mentality to address a 60's real-ity. Its bungling attempts to control off-campus political activity combined with its inability to recognize the legitimacy and depth of student feelings would unite factions as diverse as Young Republicans for Goldwater with the Young People's Socialist League and eventually lead to the massive pro-tests that would paint Berkeley as the nation's center of student activism and the New Left. Over the next three months I would spend a great deal of time listening, observing and participating in what would become known world-wide as the Free Speech Movement. As a student of politics, I was to learn much more in the streets than I did in the classroom.

What evolved was a classic no win, up-against-the-wall confrontation. The Administration would move from "all of your freedoms are removed," to "you can have some freedom," to "let's see how you like cops bashing in your heads." The Free Speech leaders would be radicalized to the point where no compromise except total victory was acceptable. Student gov-ernment and faculty solutions urging moderation and cooperation would be lost in the shuffle. Ultimately, Governor Pat Brown would send in the police and Berkeley would take on the atmosphere of a police state.

The process of alienation that had started for me with the student leader conference continued to grow, but I never made the leap from issue to ideology. It was no more in my nature to be left wing than it had been to be right wing. However, I would journey across the dividing line into civil disobedience.

Within hours of the time that Dean Katherine Towle sent out her ultimatum to campus organizations, the brother and sister team of Art and Jackie Goldberg had pulled together activist organizations ranging in orientation from the radical to conservative, and a nascent FSM was born. Shortly thereafter, the mimeographs were humming and students were buried in an avalanche of leaflets as they walked on to campus. I read mine is disbelief. The clash I had warned of a year earlier had arrived. There was no joy in being right.

As soon as it became apparent that the Administration had no intention of backing off from its new rules, the FSM leadership determined to challenge the University. Organizations were encouraged to set up card tables in the Sather Gate area to solicit support for off campus causes. I had stopped by a table to pick up some literature when a pair of deans approached and started writing down names of the folks manning the tables. Our immediate reaction was to form a line so we could have our names taken as well. The deans refused to accommodate us. The Administration's objective was to pick off and separate the leadership of the FSM from the general student body.

A few days later I came out of class to find a police car parked in Sproul Plaza surrounded by students. The police, with encouragement from the Administration, had arrested Jack Weinberg, a non-student organizer for CORE who had been soliciting support for his organization. Someone had found a bullhorn and people were making speeches from the top of the police car while Jack sat inside. I situated myself on the edge of the fountain next to the Student Union and idly scratched the head of a German Short Haired Pointer named Ludwig while I listened. Ludwig visited campus daily and played in the water. He'd become a Berkeley regular.

Eventually I stood up and joined those on the edge of the crowd thereby becoming a part of the blockade. It was my first ever participation in civil disobedience. It was a small step. There would be plenty of time for more critical thinking if the police showed up in force. Being only semi-radical, I did duty between classes and took breaks for eating and sleep. Eventually, after a couple of days, the FSM negotiated a deal with the Administration. Jack was booked on campus and turned loose, as was the police car. A collection was taken up to pay for minor damages the police car had sustained in the line of duty while serving as a podium. I threw in a dollar. Weinberg, by the way, was the one who coined the rallying cry of youth in the 60s: "Never trust anyone over 30."

The situation did not improve. Each time a solution seemed imminent, the Administration would renege or the FSM would increase its demands. In addition to the right to organize on campus, the disciplining of FSM leaders became a central issue. Demonstrations took place almost daily and were blasted in the press, which wasn't surprising considering the local press was the Oakland Tribune. I learned a great deal about media sensationalism and biased reporting. One day I would sit in on a very democratic and spirited discussion of the pros and cons of a specific action and the next day I would read in the Tribune or San Francisco Examiner that I had participated in a major insurrection of left leaning radicals who were challenging the very basis of law and order and civilized society.

Older adults, looking suspiciously like plain-clothes policemen or FBI agents, became a common occurrence on Campus. It was easy to become paranoid. If we signed a petition, demonstrated, made a speech or just stood by listening, would our pictures and names end up in some mysterious Washington file that proclaimed our disloyalty to the nation? These weren't idle thoughts. A few years earlier people's careers had been ended and lives ruined because someone had implied they were soft on communism. J. Edgar Hoover was known for tracking Civil Rights' leaders and maintaining extensive files on every aspect of their lives. While we weren't up against the KGB, caution was advisable. We looked warily at those who didn't look like us. One day a small dog was making his way around the edge of the daily demonstration, sniffing people.

"See that Chihuahua?" Jo whispered in my ear. I nodded yes. "It's a police dog in disguise. Any moment it is going to unzip its front and a German Shepherd will pop out."

The wolf in sheep's clothing was amongst us. It was a light moment to counter a serious time. And we were very serious. I sometimes wondered when the celebrated fun of being a college student would kick in.

One day I was faced with a test more serious than any I had ever faced in the classroom. On Friday, December 3, 1964, FSM leaders called for a massive sit in at Sproul Hall. Once again communication had broken down and the Administration was back peddling, caught between students and faculty on the one side and increasing pressure from the outside on the other. I thought about the implications of the sit-in and decided to join. It was partly on whim, and partly because I had a need to act. For three months I had listened to pros and cons and watched the press blatantly misrepresent what was happening on campus. I was angry, knowing that the public had little option but to believe we were being manipulated by a small group of radicals and had no legitimate concerns.

It was not wrong to utilize an edge of campus for discussing the central issues of the day, or for organizations to raise funds for supporting various causes, or even to recruit students to participate in efforts to change the community. It didn't disrupt my education. I was free to stop and listen, to join in, or pass on. What it did do was irritate powerful, established members of the community. And for that reason, our freedoms had been curtailed.

Maybe if enough students joined together and the stakes were raised high enough, the Administration would listen, the press would dig a little deeper, and our basic freedoms would be returned. I told Jo Ann I was going inside and then joined the thousand or so students who had made similar decisions. It was early in the afternoon and we were in high spirits. I believed it would be hard for the Administration to claim 1000 students were a small group of rabble-rousers bent on destroying the system. And I was right. They claimed we were a large group of rabble-rousers bent on destroying the system.

Inside I was treated to one of the more unique experiences of my life. The sit-in was well organized. Mario and other FSM leaders gave us directions on what to do if the police arrived. There were clear instructions that we were not to block doorways. The normal business of the University was not to be impeded, and we were not to be destructive in any way. Floors were organized for different purposes. The basement was set aside as the Free University where graduate students were teaching a variety of classes. These included normal topics such as physics and biology and more exotic subjects such as the nature of God. One floor was set aside as a study hall and was kept quiet. Another floor featured entertainment— including old Laurel and Hardy films.

After administrators left, the Dean's desk became a podium for speech making. I felt compelled to participate. There was a long line of speakers. We were required to take off our shoes so the desk wouldn't be damaged. The real treat though was an impromptu concert by Joan Baez. I joined a small group sitting around her in the hallway and sang protest songs. The hit of the night was "We Shall Overcome." It provided us with a sense of identification with struggles taking place in the South. I felt like I belonged and was part of something much larger than myself. Mainly I walked around and listened, taking extensive notes on what I saw and felt. Later I would sit in the Café Med and write them up. They would become the basis of talks I would give back home over the Christmas break.

Along about midnight I started thinking about my comfortable bed back in the apartment. The marble floors of Sproul Hall did not make for a good night's sleep and it appeared the police weren't coming, at least in the immediate future. Yawning, I left the building and headed home. I would come back in the morning.

I did, but I came back to a semi-police state. We had an occupied campus. Armed men in uniforms formed a cordon around the Administration Building where students were being dragged down the stairs and loaded into police vans. Windows had been taped over so people or media could not see what was transpiring inside. The great liberal governor of California had acted to "end the anarchy and maintain law and order in California."

I am sure Laurel and Hardy would have seen something to laugh about. Dragging kids down stairs on their butts while their heads bounced along behind could easily have been a scene in one of the old Keystone Cop films. The Oakland police weren't nearly as funny as the Keystone Cops, however. As for Clark Kerr, President of the University, he felt we were getting what we deserved and argued that the FSM leaders and their followers "are now finding in their effort to escape the gentle discipline of the University, they have thrown themselves into the arms of the less understanding discipline of the community at large."

Later Kerr claimed he had an understanding with Governor Brown to let the students remain in Sproul Hall over night. He would talk with the protesters in the morning in an effort to end the sit-in peacefully. But Brown reneged on the agreement. One report was that Edwin Meese, Ronald Reagan's future Attorney General and, at the time, Oakland's Deputy DA and FBI liaison, had called Brown in the middle of the night with the claim that student's were destroying the Dean's office.

I had participated in the "destruction," i.e. stood on the Dean's desk in my socks. Either the DA had received an erroneous report or he had deliberately lied to the Governor. My sense was that the right wing of American politics, which Meese represented, had much more to gain from violent confrontations than it did from negotiated settlements.

The campus came to a grinding halt and a great deal of fence sitting ended. Whole departments shut down in strike. Sproul Hall plaza filled with several thousand students in protest of the police presence. When the police made a flying wedge to grab a speaker system FSM was using, we were electrified and protected the system with our bodies. It was the closest I have ever come to being in a riot; thousands of thinking, caring students teetered on the edge of becoming an infuriated, unthinking mob. Violence and bloodshed, egged on by police action, would have been the result. Kerr, Brown, Knowland and company would have had the anarchy they were claiming, after the fact. A few days later we were to come close again.

Kerr, in a series of around the clock meetings with a select committee of Department Chairs, had arrived at a compromise he felt would provide for the extended freedom being demanded on campus while also diffusing the outside pressure to crack open student heads. Sit-in participants arrested in the Sproul Hall would be left to the tender mercies of the outside legal system and not disciplined by the University. Rights to free speech and organization on campus would be restored as long as civil disobedience was not advocated.

Kerr and Robert Scalapino, Chair of the Political Science Department, presented the compromise to a hastily called all-campus meeting of 15,000 students and faculty at the Greek Theater. There was to be no discussion and no other speakers. When Mario Savio approached the podium following the presentation, he was grabbed by police, thrown down, and dragged off the stage. Apparently he had wanted to announce a meeting in Sproul Plaza to discuss Kerr's proposal. Once again, Berkeley teetered on the edge of a riot. We moved from silent, shocked disbelief to shouting our objections. Mario, released from the room where he was held captive, urged us to stay calm and leave the area. We did, but Kerr's compromise had become compromised.

A full meeting of the Academic Senate was to be held the next day and the whole campus waited in anticipation to hear what stand Berkeley's faculty would take. We knew that most faculty members deplored the presence of police on campus and the violent way they had responded to the nonviolent demonstrators. Dragging Mario off the stage had not helped the Administration's case. Some departments such as math, philosophy, anthropology and English were clearly on the side of FSM while others including business and engineering were in opposition.

My own department of political science was clearly divided. Some professors believed that nonviolent civil disobedience threatened the stability of government. Others recognized how critical it was for helping the powerless gain power. To them, having large blocks of disenfranchised, alienated people in America seemed to be a greater threat to democracy than civil disobedience.

The Senate met on December 8 in Wheeler Hall, ironically in the same auditorium where Peter Odegard had lectured on the meaning of democracy to my Poly Sci 1 class during my first day at Berkeley. Some 5000 of us gathered outside to wait for the results and listen to the proceedings over a loud speaker.

To the students who had fought so hard and risked so much, and to those of us who had joined their cause, the results were close to euphoric. On a vote of 824-115 the faculty voted that all disciplinary actions prior to December 8 should be dropped, that students should have the right to organize on campus for off-campus political activity, and that the University should not regulate the content of speech or advocacy. Two weeks later, the Regents confirmed the faculty position.

We had won. Our freedom of speech, our freedom to organize, and our freedom to participate in the critical issue of the day were returned. While we were still a part of the future so popular with commencement speakers, we were also a part of the now, helping to shape that future.

I was curious about the background of the students who were arrested, considering I had almost been one. A sociologist was doing a study on who was involved so I volunteered to take part. We were given extensive questionnaires, trained and told to hit the streets. I seemed to inherit some of the more elusive, fringe types who always hang around Berkeley. Just finding them was an adventure.

When our data was analyzed, what we found was that a quarter or so of the participants were relatively hard corps in terms of having been actively involved in the Civil Rights movement. Most of the participants resembled me— students and grad students who were somewhat idealistic, angry at the Administration, in sympathy with the Civil Rights movement and committed to our right to participate in the political process.

Were there truly radical students on campus who saw the protests as an end, as a way to radicalize students and achieve objectives beyond retrieving the basic rights that had been taken away? Yes. I met some when I decided to help create a Free Student Union. A union made sense to me. The student government, by its very nature, was tied too closely to the Administration to be truly independent. A union would go beyond the temporary, nonrepresentational nature of the FSM and give us ongoing power and representation that we lacked as individuals.

I participated in two or three meetings including one I hosted at our apartment. Chaos was good, I quickly learned. Policemen dragging students down stairs and bashing an occasional head was to our advantage. It created solidarity among the ranks and radicalized the student body. We needed to goad the Administration into further action, the more outrageous the better.

The strategy did not reflect who I was or my goals. After sharing my opinion on what I thought about the chosen strategies, I parted ways with the Free Student Union. Apparently, most students shared my perspective. The union, to my knowledge, was not able to get off the ground.

By spring, the Campus had more or less returned to normal, that is, what represented normal at Berkeley. I was amused to read a Junior Class party announcement in the "Daily Californian."

"Everyone is welcome at our TGIF party, especially the FSM: it will give them a chance to quench their thirst." Dennis O'Shea, Junior Class Activities Chairman was quoted. "It promises to be the hell raiser of the year— lots of girls, a screaming rock and roll band that frequently plays for the Hell's Angels, and 150 gallons of liquid refreshments."

I can imagine that the Administration was praying for a return to the good old days when a 'hell raiser' was defined as an ocean of beer and a rock and roll band that played for the Hell's Angels. As for me, my interest in what was happening politically in the US had been supplanted with a growing interest in what was happening internationally. I changed my political science focus to International Relations with a concentration on comparative communism and African studies. Both seemed to have potential for some type of career path in foreign affairs.

It was at this time that the Peace Corps caught my attention. It was hard to imagine a better way to satisfy my desire to wander, provide hands-on overseas experience for a future career, and possibly do some good. Joining the Peace Corps would also answer the growingly urgent question about what I would do in June.

I did have another option. In the spring of 1965, Uncle Sam was looking for recruits. He'd bought a used colonial war from the French and needed soldiers to fight it. As a 22-year-old male about to graduate from college, I was a prime candidate.

CHAPTER 6

VIETNAM— A WAR
THAT WAS BORN UGLY

The conflict in Vietnam dated back to 1946. It was born ugly. France had lost her colonial empire in Indochina to Japan during World War II and Charles de Gaulle wanted it back. The Vietnamese Marxist Ho Chi Minh wanted independence. The Indo-China War was the result. In hope of expanding their influence, Russia and China sided with Ho Chi Minh. NATO and the US jumped in to thwart the Communist powers and support France.

In 1954 the Geneva Accords divided Indochina into four countries: North Vietnam, South Vietnam, Laos and Cambodia. Under President Eisenhower, the US replaced France in the fight against North Vietnam by providing 'military advisors' and financial aid to the politically corrupt regime of Ngo Dinh Diem in South Vietnam. Over the next ten years our support continued to grow. John Kennedy dramatically expanded the effort by increasing the number of military advisers from 700 to 15,000.

By the time I was ready to graduate from Berkeley, Lyndon Johnson was ready to send in the troops. The Cold War was raging. America's leaders saw Vietnam as a critical step in stopping the spread of communism. Lose Vietnam, the Domino Theory argued, and all of Southeast Asia would follow.

My political science professors in International Relations at UC Berkeley had a different perspective. Communism was changing. It was no longer monolithic in nature but had taken on nationalistic flavors. Communism in Russia was different from communism in China. The Russians were as fearful of Chinese massing on their border as they were of the US's nuclear weapons.

One day I arrived at my class on Comparative Communism and learned my professor had been invited to Washington to provide advice on Vietnam. The message he carried was that Ho Chi Minh was a nationalist first and a Marxist second. He wanted to reunite North and South Vietnam. He was no more interested in being dominated by Russia or China than he had been in being dominated by France. Becoming involved in a full-scale war was not in the best interest of the United States and might prove to be a costly mistake.

Washington refused to listen. America's leaders had grown up on a steady diet of Cold War rhetoric. Not even the insanity of McCarthyism had shaken their faith. Being 'soft on communism' was political suicide. When Khrushchev banged his shoe on his desk at the United Nations and said he would bury us, we banged back.

Lyndon Johnson and his closest advisers believed in the communist threat but there was more. America was the leader of the Free World (with free, as in the case of the Diem brothers, rather loosely defined as anti-communist). Our image was involved. Lose Vietnam and we would lose prestige. Johnson, with his Texas-size ego, took the matter personally. We would not lose Vietnam on his watch.

But I was convinced there was more to the fight in Vietnam than a communist grab for power. The focus of my studies on Africa in 1965 was about the struggle for independence from colonial powers. I felt Ho Chi Minh was involved in a similar fight.

A huge rally was held on campus in May. It was one of the first major Anti-Vietnam protests in the nation. I went to listen. Dozens of speakers including Irving Stone, Dr. Spock of baby fame, Senator Gruening from Alaska and Norman Mailer spoke out against the war. Later the House Un-American Activities Committee targeted the event's organizers. If Vietnam was part of a communist plot to take over the world, then dissent in the U.S. against the war was part of that plot. The same FBI agents who had prowled on the fringes of the earlier Free Speech Movement were undoubtedly prowling the edges of the protest, taking pictures and taking names.

In some ways, the rally was like a circus. Over 30,000 students and anti-war activists participated. Folks from throughout the Bay Area poured on to Union Field and there were lots of interesting people in the Bay Area. Haight Asbury and the hippie era was still a year off, but the elements were all in place. I was standing on Bancroft Avenue when a crazily painted bus drove up and stopped. Out piled a group of people who were dressed in outrageous outfits and had their faces painted. They danced by me, apparently high on something.

"It's Ken Kesey and his Merry Pranksters, a more 'with-it' girl standing next to me explained. "Neal Cassady drives the bus."

Cassady had been part of the Beat Generation and a friend of Jack Kerouac. He had been immortalized as Dean Moriarty in "On the Road." His connection with Ken Kesey and the Merry Pranksters would introduce another type of trip to him: LSD. Tom Wolfe's book, "*The Electric Kool-Aid Acid Test*," chronicled the experience of the Merry Pranksters on their gaily-painted bus named Further on its psychedelic journey across the US.

What I had learned about Vietnam in my classes and at events like the protest created a dilemma for me, as it did for most young men of my generation. If drafted, I would go. I couldn't imagine burning my draft card, running off to Canada, or hiding out in the National Guard. I actually believe we owe our country service. But fighting in a war I didn't believe in and killing people I didn't want to kill was at the very bottom of the list of what I wanted to do when I graduated. And there was more. I am allergic to taking orders and can't stand being yelled at. I'd make a lousy soldier. I saw a court-martial in my future.

Luckily, Peace Corps Recruiters were coming to Berkeley and Peace Corps was something I truly wanted to do. I could serve America in my own way. Peace Corps service would not eliminate my military obligation but it might buy time for the Vietnam conflict to end.

CHAPTER 7

THE FBI AND PEACE CORPS ARE TOLD I AM A COMMUNIST

I discussed joining the Peace Corps with my fiancée. "Let's do it!" Jo Ann responded. She and I would go together as a husband and wife team. When the Peace Corps recruiters opened their booth in front of the Berkeley Student Union in February, we were there to greet them.

"Sign us up," we urged.

"Fill these out," the recruiter responded, handing us two umpteen page blue applications. "You will also have to pass a language aptitude test in Kurdish and provide letters of recommendation." I had my doubts about the Kurdish.

Apparently we looked good on paper. In a few weeks the Peace Corps informed us that we had been tentatively selected to serve as teachers in Liberia, West Africa. My brain did a jig. The age-old question of what you do when you graduate from school and enter the real world had been answered, or at least postponed.

Uncle Sam with his growing hunger for bodies to fight the Vietnam War would have to wait.

There were still hurdles to jump. They were tied to the illusive *if*. We could go *if* we could get through the background security check, *if* we weren't deselected during training, and *if* we could pass the physical. Training wasn't a worry. We had enough confidence in ourselves to assume we would float through. How hard could it be after Berkeley?

The Security Check was something else. Jo Ann was squeaky clean but I had been up to mischief at Berkeley, hung out with the wrong people, been seen in a few places where law-abiding people weren't supposed to be, and had my name on a number of petitions.

"And where were you, Mr. Mekemson, the night the students took over the Administration Building?"

Maybe there was even a file somewhere; maybe it was labeled Radical. J. Edgar Hoover saw Red when he looked at Berkeley.

Soon I started hearing from friends. The man with the badge had been by to see them. The background security check was underway. One day I came home to the apartment and found my roommate Jerry there. He was pale and agitated. His eyes bounced around the room.

"I have to talk to you Curtis," he blurted out. "The FBI was by today doing your Peace Corps background check and I told them you had been holding communist cell meetings in our apartment."

Jerry was deadly serious; Jerry was dead.

"What in the hell are you talking about?" I yelled, seeing all of our hopes dashed and me rotting in jail. As I've noted, being accused of communist leanings in the 60s was a very dangerous accusation. I knew that Jerry disagreed with me over my involvement in Berkeley's Free Speech Movement and probably disagreed with me over the Vietnam War, but I hadn't a clue on how deep that disagreement went. Or what he based his information on.

My degree in International Relations had included a close look at Communism. I found nothing attractive about repressive totalitarian states. The closest I came to joining a leftist group had been the Free Student Union. But I had severed my relationship with the organization.

I was not happy with Jerry that night or for some time after. I assumed the Peace Corps option was out and begin thinking of alternatives. They were bleak. As it turned out, we received final notification from the Peace Corps a few weeks later. We were accepted. Jerry could live. The people who said good things about me must have outweighed the people who said bad things. Either that or Jo looked so good they didn't want to throw the babe out with the bath water. Or possibly the majority of other students who signed up for the Peace Corps from Berkeley in 1965 had rap sheets similar to mine.

There was one final hitch. I was to report to the Army Induction Center in Oakland for my Peace Corps' physical. It was an experience not worth repeating. I lined up with a bunch of naked men to be poked and prodded.

"Turn your head and cough. Now, bend over."

I took it like a man and escaped as soon as the opportunity presented itself. A couple of days later I came back from class and there was a scribbled note from my other roommate, Cliff, who was also going into the Peace Corps.

"The Induction Center called," he wrote, "and there is a problem with your urinalysis." I was to call them.

"Damn," I thought. "Why is this so difficult?" So I called the Center and resigned myself to peeing in another jar. With really good luck, I might avoid the naked-man line.

I got a very cooperative secretary who quickly bounced me to a very cooperative nurse who quickly bounced me to a very cooperative technician who quickly bounced me to a very cooperative doctor— and none of them could find any record of my errant urinalysis. They didn't see any problems and they didn't know who had called. They suggested I call back later and be bounced around again. More than a little worried, I rushed off to my next class.

That evening I reported my lack of success to Cliff. He got this strange little smile on his face and asked me what day it was.

"April 1st," I replied as recognition of having been seriously screwed dawned in my mind. "You little ass!" I screamed, as Cliff shot for the door with me in fast pursuit. He made it to Telegraph Avenue before I caught him. The damage wasn't all that bad, considering.

The day before Cliff sent me scurrying after the errant urinalysis, Sargent Shriver arrived on campus. I, along with several thousand other students, flocked to hear him speak.

John Kennedy recruited his brother-in-law in 1961 to set up and then head the Peace Corps. "If it flops," Kennedy had said, "it will be easier to fire a relative than a political friend." The President had first proposed the concept to a crowd of 5,000 students during a campaign speech at the University of Michigan on October 14, 1960. He was running four hours late and it was two in the morning. The response was overwhelming. Kennedy saw the organization as an important way to win friends in third world countries and counter similar efforts being made by the Chinese and Russians. One of his first acts as President in 1961 was to create the agency. He gave Shriver one month to do the job.

By 1965 when I joined the Peace Corps, Kennedy had been assassinated and the Peace Corps had become one of the most popular foreign relation programs in US history. Shriver's appearance at UC Berkeley that spring was a big deal. He still carried the aura of the Kennedy years. In addition to heading up the Peace Corps, he now headed up LBJ's massive War on Poverty. Berkeley was also important to Shriver. We had provided more Volunteers than any other college in the nation.

"First of all, I am in favor of free speech," he began. "Even the initials FSM don't scare me. Back in Washington my enemies say they stand for "Fire Shriver Monday." But LBJ says they stand for "Find Shriver Money.""

He captured us. Berkeley's Free Speech Movement had dominated our lives. Times had been serious, even dangerous. We were ready to laugh.

"But here on campus," he went on, "I want to talk about today's challenge to the young, to the American university student of the 60s… of what I think might be called a "free service movement."

Shriver then used a quote from Bob Rupley, a 1962 Berkeley graduate and Peace Corps Volunteer, to describe what he felt the essence of the Peace Corps was:

"Apathy, ignorance and disorganization are the things we want to eliminate… in all areas in which we work. Clearly no Volunteer can hope for absolute success, nor can he even expect limited success to come easily. Clearly, the Peace Corps is not the responsibility of every American. And it shouldn't be! In many ways, the life of a Volunteer who sincerely seeks to effect progress is miserable."

Three weeks after making this statement, Rupley was shot to death in Caracas, Venezuela while he was working as Peace Corps staff.

Shriver told us the Peace Corps was looking for unreasonable men and women. Reasonable people accept the status quo. Unreasonable people seek to change it. We were noted for being unreasonable at Berkeley.

"You have demonstrated your leadership in the generation of the '60s,' the generation that will not take 'yes' for an answer, which has shown an unwillingness to accept the pat answers of society— either in Berkeley, in Selma or in Caracas, Venezuela," Shriver noted.

"Once in every generation," he went on to say, " fundamentals are challenged and the entire fabric of our life is taken apart seam by seam and reconstructed… Such a time is now again at hand and it is clear that many of you are unreasonable men (and women), restless, questioning, challenging, taking nothing for granted."

We had not forfeited our rights at Berkeley, nor had we, according to Shriver, forfeited our claim to a fellowship with the Peace Corps. And this, at least in part, was why I had been accepted as a Volunteer. Participation in the Free Speech Movement was regarded as a plus, not a minus.

But, according to Shriver, the time had come to move beyond protest. He concluded his talk with a ringing call for service.

"We ask all of you who have taken what you have learned about our society and made it live… to join us in the politics of service, to demonstrate to the poor and the forgotten of villages and slums in America and the world what you have learned of Democracy and freedom and equality. The times demand no less."

"It is time not just to speak, but to serve."

We stood and gave Shriver a standing ovation and I knew that joining the Peace Corps had been the right decision for me.

CHAPTER 8

THE DEAD CHICKEN DANCE

Graduation from Berkeley, marriage in Auburn, a three-day honeymoon in Monterey, and reporting for Liberia VI Peace Corps training at San Francisco State College transpired in one whirlwind week.

My best man, Frank Martin, played his role superbly— from hosting the bachelor party at the Diamond Springs Hotel to making sure our escape car was appropriately decorated. Frank grew up with me in Diamond Springs, California. We had also attended Sierra College together. Somewhere along the line he had discovered he was gay. Later on, he and his partner Hank hosted several offbeat but elegant anniversary parties for us at their home on Clay Street in San Francisco.

Given our three-day honeymoon, Jo and I figured we would hold the record for newlyweds arriving at Peace Corps training. But we didn't. One couple spent their honeymoon night flying out to San Francisco State University. ("Gee, Hon, let's check out the airplane's toilet again.")

Upon arrival, the married couples were crammed into one wing of Merced Hall, a student dormitory. Tiny rooms, paper-thin walls and a communal bathroom became our new home. We soon knew a lot about each other.

Peace Corps staff wanted to know even more; Beebo, the psychologist, was assigned to follow us around and take notes. First, however, they pumped us full of gamma globulin and explained 'deselection.' Our job was to decide whether Peace Corps was something we really wanted to do. Their job was to provide stress to help make the decision. Initially this came in the form of a SF State football coach hired to shape us up.

"Okay you guys, let's see how fast you can run up and down the stadium steps five times!" I hadn't liked that particular sport during my brief football career in high school— and still didn't.

Beyond mini-boot camp, our time was filled with attending classes designed to teach us about Liberia and elementary school education. We were even given a stint at practice teaching in South San Francisco. There wasn't much for Beebo to write about. In case he missed anything, we were given a battery of psychological tests to probe our miscellaneous neuroses. These were followed by in-depth interviews.

"Answer honestly. Say the first thing that pops into your mind." Yeah, sure I will.

A few people did wash out and were whisked away. Naturally it was a topic of conversation. What had they done wrong? Were we next?

The true stress test was supposed to be a camping trip up in the Sierras. This may have been true for the kids straight out of the Bronx who had rarely seen stars much less slept out in the woods, but Jo and I considered it a vacation. We had been raised in the foothills of the Sierras and were going home. The ante was upped considerably when the camp leader arrived the first night.

"Here's dinner," he announced casually as he unloaded a crate of live chickens from the back of his pickup. They clucked a greeting.

Fortunately, I had chopped off a few chicken heads in my youth and knew about such things as chicken plucking and gutting. I couldn't appear too eager in the chopping department, though. Beebo might write something like "displays obvious psychopathic tendencies."

Lizzie Borden would have been proud of me. "Close the door, lock and latch it, here comes Curt with a brand new hatchet!"

My chicken spurted blood from its neck and performed a jerky little death dance, turning the city boys and girls a chalky white. Their appetites made a quick exit in pursuit of their color when I reached inside a still warm Henny Penny to yank out her slippery innards. It seemed that my fellow trainees were lacking in intestinal fortitude. If so, it was fine with me; I got more chicken.

Beebo's biggest day came when we faced the wilderness obstacle course. Our first challenge was to cross a bouncy rope bridge over a deep gorge. Beebo stood nearby, scratching away on his pad. We then rappelled down a cliff— scratch, scratch, scratch. Our every move was to be scrutinized and subjected to psychological analysis. We rebelled.

"Beebo, you've been following us around and taking notes for two months. Now it's your turn. See that cliff. Climb down it."

"Uh, no."

"Beebo, you don't understand," we were laughing, "you have to take your turn."

Reluctantly, very reluctantly, Beebo agreed. About half way down he froze and became glued to the rock with all of the tenacity of a tick on a hound. We tried to talk him down, and we tried to talk him up. We even tried talking him sideways. Nothing worked. Finally we climbed up and hauled him down. Note taking was finished. We wrapped up our wilderness week and our training was complete. Jo Ann and I took the oath and became official Peace Corps Volunteers.

We were allowed one week at home to complete any unfinished business before flying to New York City and reporting to the Pan Am desk at JFK. Since there wasn't much to do, Jo and I relaxed and recovered from our tumultuous year that had begun ever so long ago with the Free Speech Movement at Berkeley.

We wrapped up our brief visit with a going away party in Jo Ann's back yard in Auburn. Surrounded by friends and family, we talked into the night. It was one of those perfect summer evenings that California is famous for, complete with a warm breeze tainted with a hint of honeysuckle flowers.

CHAPTER 9

LEFT BEHIND AND VERY ALONE

Our cross-country flight ended as the jet bounced down on the runway at JFK. We stood up and joined the crowd jostling to get out, two country kids who had traveled a long way from rural Northern California. All we had to do was check in at the Pan Am desk, grab a bite to eat, and catch our trans-Atlantic flight to Africa.

Ah, that life should be so simple. We managed to find the Pan Am desk all right, but no one was there.

"Excuse me, could you tell me where the Liberia Peace Corps group is?" I asked a harried attendant.

"I don't have any idea," came the brusque reply.

Have you ever had the sinking feeling that you have blown something critically important? It starts with the hair on your head and works its way downward to your toes. Every part of your body jumps in to let you know you aren't nearly as smart as you imagine you are. It's the stomach that serves as the real messenger, however, and mine was rolling like the Atlantic in a category 5 hurricane.

"Check the instructions again, Curt," the voice of reason standing beside me directed. Good idea.

"Well, it says right here we are supposed to be at the Pan Am desk no later than 5:00 p.m." It was only 4:00. My stomach calmed down to a respectable jet engine rumble. "Let's have a bite and then check back." I suggested, working hard to be the man.

Five o'clock came and no one, nothing, nada; it was serious panic time. "Wait here, Jo, in case anyone comes. I'll go check the instructions one more time."

We had stuffed our bags in a drop-a-quarter-in-the-slot storage locker while we ate. I freed my shoulder bag from captivity and reread the instructions. Yes, we were in the right place at the right time. Then there it was, *the answer*, staring at me in black and white. "You will fly to New York on August 7th."

It was the 8th.

Damn! I slowly climbed back up the stairs.

"I've found them, Jo Ann." A look of relief and the beginning of a smile crossed her face.

"Where are they?"

"In Liberia."

Let me say this about the two of us; we were both stubborn as mules when we thought we were right. This could create problems when we disagreed, but the potential for disaster was miniscule in comparison to when we both agreed we were right and we weren't. Reality didn't matter and certainly a little date on a piece of paper we had each read a dozen times wasn't going to deter us. The 7th was our going away party in Auburn, period. While we were kicking up our heels and smelling the honeysuckle, our compatriots were crossing the Atlantic to Africa. Now we were left behind, very alone and stuck in New York City.

"What are we going to do?" Jo asked in a shaky voice. The only thing that came to my mind was a double-vodka anything.

It was probably a good thing United Airlines had let us on the airplane in San Francisco without noticing our tickets were one day out of date. Had we called Washington from home, the Peace Corps might have suggested we stay there.

As it turned out, the Peace Corps representative sounded amused when we called the emergency number in Washington after our visit to the bar. "Do you have enough money to get through until tomorrow?" he had asked. Yes. Jo Ann's mom had insisted we take an extra hundred dollars in cash from her. "OK, call this number in the morning."

We decided to sleep in the airport to save our scant resources. It was a resolution with a short lifespan; we couldn't adjust to the bedroom. Somewhere around midnight I said, "Look, Jo, I am going to see if a cab driver will help us find a hotel we can afford." The first guy in line was a grizzled old character in a taxi of similar vintage. I told him our story. He studied me for a moment and then said, "Go get your wife, and I'll find somewhere for you."

A more cynical observer might note we were lambs waiting to be fleeced but what followed was one of those minor events that speak so loudly for the positive side of human nature. The taxi driver took care of us. He reached across the cab, turned off his meter and then drove to three different hotels. At each one he got out, went inside and talked to the manager. At the third one he came out and announced he had found our lodging.

"This place isn't fancy," he reported, "but it is clean, safe and affordable." Affordable turned out to be dirt-cheap. To this day I am sure the cab driver finessed a deal for us. Two very exhausted puppies fell into bed and deep sleep.

The Peace Corps representative we talked to the next morning wasn't nearly as friendly as the one the night before, but at least he didn't tell us we had to go home. A commercial flight to Liberia would be leaving in three days. Could we hang out in New York? Did he need to send us some money? Could we follow directions?

Yes, we could hang out; no, they didn't need to send money; and yes, we could find our way to the proper airline at the correct time on the right day. Jo and I visited New York's 1964/65 World's Fair, checked out the city and considered the three days as an extension of our all too short honeymoon.

As the old saying goes, "all's well that ends well."

CHAPTER 10

DR. LIVINGSTON, I PRESUME

We made it to the right terminal on the right day and at the right time. In fact, our paranoia insisted we be four hours early. We watched lots of planes take off and land.

Finally, we found ourselves flying over a rough Atlantic. To quote Snoopy, "it was a dark and stormy night." Lighting danced between the clouds as we made a valiant effort to deplete the airplane's complimentary booze supply. We toasted each other, we toasted the fact we had made it, we toasted Jo's mom for the hundred dollars, and we toasted Liberia.

"Good morning." The pilot's speaker driven voice woke me from my booze-induced sleep. Jo and I scrambled to look down and were met by a vast sea of green, broken occasionally by small clearings filled with round huts. Tropical Africa!

The pilot announced a brief stopover in Dakar where French-speaking Senegalese served warm Coca-Cola and stale ginger snaps. It was the type of meal you really should forget but never do. Two hours later we dropped into Robert's Field, Liberia's International Airport. The flight attendants wrenched open the door admitting a sudden blast of heat and humidity. Roaming the streets of New York City in August had prepared us for the weather but not the sight.

Striding across the tarmac to greet us was my old friend Morris Carpenter. He and I had been in student government together at Sierra College.

Morris was a year ahead of me and transferred to Chico State College at the end of my freshman year. We remained close friends via long handwritten letters. During his senior year, he joined the Peace Corps and was assigned to Liberia. His letters from Africa were part of my inspiration for joining. Little did I dream that Jo Ann and I would end up in the same country serving as Volunteers.

All grins, we tumbled into each other. I couldn't resist saying, "Dr. Livingston, I presume."

Morris had been camped out at the Peace Corps Director's office in Monrovia for a month seeking a change in assignment when our arrival had been announced. He had quickly volunteered to pick us up. The Director, recognizing an opportunity for Morris-free time, had agreed even faster.

On our way into Monrovia, Morris filled us in on his experiences. One year of living in Liberia had coated his youthful idealism with a thin veneer of cynicism.

His first assignment had been as an elementary school teacher on Bushrod Island, located next to Monrovia. That career had come to a crashing halt when he had caught the principal squeezing hot pepper juice into a young girl's eyes. Whippings were common in Liberian schools, but use of the fiery liquid was over the edge. Morris grabbed the principal's arm.

"You are a *small woman*," he angrily accused her, which is a major insult in Liberia. As it turned out, the principal was a cousin to one of Liberia's ruling elite, which made her a *big woman*. She had Morris booted out of the school within 24 hours.

Peace Corps staff was sympathetic but powerless to do anything about the principal's action. They found Morris employment as a Public Administration Volunteer in the Liberia Department of Education, where he spent a frustrating six months attempting to establish a modern filing system. It didn't happen. The Department served mainly as an income-producing opportunity for the relatives of prominent politicians. Finding files was not a required skill set.

"I couldn't get past ABC," Morris grumbled. He was much more successful at his night job: locating Monrovia's best bars and bar maids. It was time to move on.

Morris requested a rural assignment. And he got it. Peace Corps found him a job teaching at an elementary school in the small village of Yopea. It was about as rural as Peace Corps assignments went in Liberia. Getting there involved driving 130 miles upcountry on Liberia's main dirt road and then following a small dirt track for 20 miles to the tiny village consisting of twelve huts, a two-room school, and a CARE kitchen. (CARE is an international humanitarian agency that provides food and other types of aid in underdeveloped countries.)

He shared teaching responsibilities with the school's principal. His job was to teach the fourth, fifth and sixth grades. Students came from surrounding farms as well as the village. Life was much quieter and more productive than it had been in Monrovia. If it became too quiet, he escaped to Monrovia or Gbarnga on his Honda Motorcycle. Morris told us he would have been happy to finish off his Peace Corps experience in Yopea. "I liked the principal, enjoyed the kids and built a basketball court."

He didn't, however, like the Peace Corps Volunteer who was assigned to work with him a few months later. A fundamentalist from Tennessee, JC considered it his responsibility to convert the 'heathen' Liberians. This may have been appropriate behavior for a missionary, but it was inappropriate for a Peace Corps Volunteer.

The dislike was mutual. JC did not approve of Morris's lifestyle. Adding fuel to the fire, Peace Corps required that the two share a house. The close proximity didn't work. Morris wanted a divorce. JC "was just too goofy." Morris hopped on his Honda and zipped in to Gbarnga to meet with Peace Corps' upcountry staff, Bob Cohen. "I want JC out of my village," Morris demanded. Bob told him that it was only a personality clash. "Go back to work." Morris went back to Yopea all right, but he packed his bags and headed for Monrovia.

"Either find me a new assignment or send me home," he told the Liberia Peace Corps Director.

And that's where we came into the picture.

Morris dutifully dropped us off at Peace Corps headquarters in Monrovia to begin our in-country orientation and take care of miscellaneous bureaucratic chores. While Jo Ann and I had been playing at the World's Fair, our fellow volunteers had been sweltering through hours of meetings. Now it was our turn.

CHAPTER 11

LIBERIA: A NATION BORN AND NURTURED IN PARANOIA

Our in-country orientation, Morris's experience, and the training in San Francisco, all suggested Liberia's history would add a unique challenge to our jobs as Peace Corps Volunteers.

Liberia was born and nurtured in paranoia. The country's birth took place in the US during the early 1800's. The number of free black people was growing rapidly. Yankees saw this growth as an issue of assimilation and competition. Southern slave owners saw it as a dangerous threat; the increasing number of free blacks encouraged slaves to think of freedom. Insurrection was a possibility that generated deep fear in the minds of slave owners. Visions of being killed at night haunted their dreams.

Various solutions were suggested including the creation of a new state in the US strictly for free black people. Louisiana was named as one possibility. Carving a state out of western territories was another. Henry Clay, Andrew Jackson, Daniel Webster and a number of other prominent Americans offered a different solution: ship free blacks back to Africa.

The proposal was greeted with enthusiasm. Northern humanitarians believed that free blacks would be more successful in Africa. Southern slave owners felt that removing free blacks from the continent would eliminate their influence on slaves. Powerful Christian groups added their approval. They saw a new world of souls to harvest. Given this level of support, the American Colonization Society (ACS) was established in 1816 with the objective of repatriating black Americans back to Africa.

In 1820, ACS sent the first group of 88 free blacks and three white ACS agents to West Africa on the ship *Elizabeth*. Purchasing land for the colony from the reluctant African tribes was not easy. Gunboat diplomacy solved the problem. US Navy Lieutenant Robert Stockton persuaded a local tribal chief, King Peter, to sell ACS Cape Mesurado by pointing a gun at the Chief's head. Within two years, the site was named Monrovia, after President James Monroe, and the region was given the name Liberia in honor of freedom.

Life was bleak and dangerous at first. The tribal people were not happy at seeing the intruders take over their land and the America-Liberians, as they came to be known, constituted a very small percentage of the total population. Many died from disease— the new Liberians had long since lost their immunity to tropical bugs.

Further territory was added to Liberia by Stockton's successor, Jehudi Ashmun, using similar methods. In 1825 he persuaded King Peter and other tribal chiefs to sell prime real estate along the coast for 500 bars of tobacco, three barrels of rum, five casks of gun powder, five umbrellas, and miscellaneous other trinkets.

Despite the efforts of ACS, only a tiny portion of America's black population, some 17,000, emigrated from the US to Liberia. Even with the addition of Africans freed from slave ships and a small contingent of blacks from Barbados, America-Liberians continued to be a small minority in Liberia. In 1847 they declared their independence from the American Colonization Society and Liberia became the first modern black republic in Africa.

The history of Liberia is the history of the relationship between America-Liberians and the tribal people. The America-Liberians had learned their lessons well in America. They quickly set themselves up as the ruling class. Tight controls were established over the government, military, education, media and economic opportunities.

Tribal Liberians were regarded and treated as second-class citizens and possibly even slaves. In 1929 the League of Nations instigated an investigation into the use of forced, unpaid labor from Liberia on the Spanish island of Fernando Po. Prominent Americo-Liberians had directed Liberian soldiers to raid tribal villages to obtain the workers. A fee was paid for each man sent to Fernando Po. Liberia's Vice President Allan Yancey and possibly President Charles King had participated in the scheme.

Whether King was involved or not, there is no doubt he was corrupt. The 1982 Guinness Book of World Records listed his 1927 election as the "most fraudulent" in history. King received 234,000 votes at a time when Liberia only had 15,000 registered voters.

Fernando Po represented the tip of a large iceberg. Tribal people were expected to provide free labor for public projects such as road building. They were also expected to provide an inexpensive or free source of labor for the large upcountry farms of Americo-Liberians. Tribal chiefs also benefitted, as did a major American corporation.

In 1926 Liberia provided Firestone Tire and Rubber Company with a 99-year, one million acre concession to grow rubber trees. There was to be an exemption on all present and future taxes and the government guaranteed a cheap labor supply— even if soldiers had to recruit it. During my time in Liberia, Firestone workers would go on strike to earn $.25 per hour.

Power and privilege were the results of the policies of the Americo-Liberian government. But the power and privilege were accompanied by an underlying fear that the majority native population would rise up in revolt. This in turn, ironically, led to a siege mentality among Americo-Liberians similar in nature to that felt by the white slave owners in the Southern United States.

When Jo Ann and I arrived in August 1965, Peace Corps' role was to help bring Liberia's tribal population into the twentieth century. It was a first for the country, considering that Americo-Liberians had worked so long to keep the tribal population under tight control.

The times 'they were a changing,' however, as Bob Dylan sang. Independence was sweeping through the continent as one country after another threw off its colonial chains. Liberia's tribal people were aware of what was happening in the world around them, and the natives were getting restless.

On an outward level, we found a number of similarities between the United States and Liberia. English was the national language, the currency of the country was well-worn American dollars, and the flag was red, white and blue, complete with eleven stripes and one star. We even learned that the commanding general of the Liberian army was named George Washington. Both the government and the judiciary appeared to be patterned after the American system.

In reality, Liberia was a one party state. The government was controlled by the True Whig Party, which in turn was controlled by Americo-Liberians. What justice existed was heavily weighted toward keeping the Americo-Liberians in power. The challenge to William Shradrack Tubman, who had been President since 1943, was to convince the tribal people they were getting a good deal, make a show of it internationally, and still protect the privileges of the Americo-Liberians. This required an incredible balancing act at which Tubman was a master. The recipe for success involved one part substance, five parts fancy footwork, and ten parts paranoia. The paranoia evolved from the fear that the tribal Liberians would take the process seriously and demand their share or, God forbid, all of the goodies.

As long as Peace Corps Volunteers behaved themselves, they were part of the improvements Tubman was offering to the tribal people. The Liberian government made it quite clear that there would be serious consequences for anyone caught challenging the supremacy of the Americo-Liberians and the True Whig Party. For Liberians, the serious consequences could mean jail, or worse. For us, serious consequences would include a one-way ticket out of the country.

I would find myself on the edge of being shipped out, twice.

CHAPTER 12

ARMIES OF THE NIGHT

Bob and Gerry Branch, friends from training in San Francisco, generously volunteered to host our stay in Monrovia. They lived in a second floor apartment that overlooked one of Monrovia's busiest streets. We had a bird's-eye view of life in the city.

Monrovia was bursting at the seams with young people escaping from rural areas. Poverty was intense. Tin shacks fought for space as extended families struggled to find shelter from tropical downpours. Taxi and money-bus drivers, using their horns for brakes, competed with mangy dogs in creating unceasing noise. Air was tainted with the unique smell of cooked palm oil, smoke and rotting garbage.

On the plus side, Monrovia had several good restaurants, a modern movie theater, an air-conditioned supermarket and a large paperback bookstore, all of which we came to appreciate over the next two years.

Most Americo-Liberians did quite well and the top families lived in luxury. They owned mansions in Monrovia and large farms upcountry. Many had second homes overseas. Their children went to college in Europe and America and dressed in the latest fashions. President Tubman's official residence, located on the edge of town, had cost the Liberian people $15 million (approximately $120 million in today's dollars).

We were quite relieved to learn that our teaching jobs weren't in Monrovia. Originally, we had been assigned to an elementary school down the coast in Buchanan. It came with golden beaches and swaying palm trees. Staff told us our top rating in training had earned us the assignment. We weren't even aware that we had been "rated."

Naturally another couple grabbed the assignment when we failed to turn up on time. We were left with their jobs; Jo would teach first grade and I would teach second in the upcountry town of Gbarnga. Evidently, this was our punishment for partying too long in Auburn. Gbarnga was a long 120 miles out of Monrovia on the nation's primary dirt road. With a population approaching 5000, it was Liberia's largest upcountry town and the center of government for Bong County.

We were eager to get there and escaped from Monrovia as soon as the Director said go. Wellington Sirleaf, the Peace Corps' driver, carted our minimal belongings and us up to our new home. We arrived in Gbarnga just before dark— tired, hungry, and nervous. Our feelings ran the gamut from "Wow, we are finally here," to "What in the heck have we gotten ourselves into?"

What Gbarnga had that other upcountry sites lacked, however, was an official Peace Corps staff person, Bob Cohen, and an official Peace Corps doctor, Less Cohen (not related). I assumed this would make our life 'officially' easier. Sirleaf took us straight to Bob's trailer. It was located on a well-maintained USAID (United States Agency for International Development) compound. Bob came out to greet us.

"Welcome to Gbarnga," he said. "Your house is located across town."

Using mental telepathy, I beamed to him, "Invite us in for dinner. It's the proper thing to do."

"The Volunteers had a work party and cleaned your house last week," he went on, oblivious to my sending. I urged Jo Ann to look hungry. "And, they even drew you a bucket of water."

This seemed to impress Bob, so I mumbled something like, "They shouldn't have."

"Wellington will drive you over so you can get settled in. Enjoy your evening." And with that, Bob returned to his trailer. I pictured his filet mignon getting cold.

There was one more stop before we got to our new home. This time it was to see Shirley Penchef, another Peace Corps Volunteer. She was waiting at her house with a young Liberian of the Kpelle tribe and a surprise. It wasn't food.

"This is Sam," she bubbled (Shirley always bubbled). "Sam is so excited you are here! He has been waiting weeks for you! He is going to be your houseboy!"

Jo and I were speechless. We had talked about the possibility; it was common practice among Peace Corps Volunteers. A young Liberian would help with chores, earn spending money, and often eat with the volunteer. Both the Liberian and the Volunteer gained from the experience. We recognized the value of the arrangement but had decided that having a houseboy didn't fit the Peace Corps image.

I mean, how do you tell the folks back home you are roughing it out here in the jungle and doing 'good' while someone cooks your dinner, washes your clothes and cuts your grass? On the other hand, how do you tell a woman who talks in exclamation points and a 13 year old boy who is grinning from ear to ear that you don't want what they are selling?

"Uh, gee, uh, well, why doesn't Sam help us get settled in and then we'll see," we managed to stutter. It was one of the better decisions we were to make in Liberia.

"It's time to go," Wellington announced impatiently. I surmised that a delicious plate of hot Liberian food was waiting for him somewhere in Gbarnga as soon as he could lose us. Sam, Jo Ann and I climbed in the jeep, waved goodbye to Shirley, and went bouncing off down the road.

I don't want to be melodramatic about the introduction to our house but a little horror movie music might be appropriate. The sun had just set when we arrived. In the tropics, that's like someone turned off the lights on a dark night. Twilight doesn't linger. Fortunately, we had a flashlight. Outward appearances weren't bad. Our new home was a typical Liberian town house. Two sets of closed shutters and a door stared out at us. A zinc roof capped the whitewashed walls. Off to the left was a hole in the ground that Sam informed us was our well. Peeking out from behind on the right was the outhouse. All in all, it was pretty much what we expected.

Then we opened the door.

It was a full scale Armies of the Night scene straight out of Hollywood, the type of scene Bella Lugosi drooled over. Our noses were assailed with the scent of something that had been entombed for a thousand years. The floor writhed with life. Hundreds of small tunnels etched their way up the walls. I jumped back a foot. Jo Ann qualified for the Olympics.

Sam laughed. "Lots of bug-a-bug and cockroaches," he observed as we peered in at the chaos.

Sure enough, our flashlight revealed that the writhing floor was a multitude of three-inch African cockroaches scurrying every which way. The tunnels climbing the walls had been sculpted by termites, or bug-a-bug as the Liberians colorfully named them. The tomb-like odor was how a house normally smells in the tropics when left vacant for a few weeks.

Bob's proudly drawn bucket of water sat carefully placed in the middle of the living room.

CHAPTER 13

THE LEVITATING SQUAT ROUTINE

The bucket of water temporarily blocked our darker visions. Warm thoughts of veteran Peace Corps Volunteers taking care of the new kids filled our minds.

I directed the flashlight into the bucket. A thick layer of scum reflected the light as a complete ecosystem came to life. Somewhere in the house, a malaria-bearing mommy mosquito was extremely proud of her progeny. Hundreds of little wigglers broke the surface, virtually guaranteeing the continuation of the family line for a thousand years.

"Can you imagine what this would have been like if the Volunteers hadn't cleaned?" I chuckled nervously, making a weak attempt at humor. Jo Ann recognized it for what it was worth and ignored me. I had the uncharitable thought that cleaning our house out had meant removing the furniture.

"Let's tour our new home." Again silence, but at least Jo Ann followed me. I had the flashlight. The bedroom was first. A fist-sized crab like spider went scurrying sidewise across the wall. *Splat!* One problem was eliminated. I hoped that its aunts, uncles, brothers and sisters weren't the vengeful type. Our bed was a moldy mattress shoved into the corner. It smelled suspiciously like the house.

"Hey, our first furniture," I noted, still trying to get a laugh. This time I was rewarded with a weak smile.

Next we came to the kitchen. It would never be featured in *Sunset Magazine*. A kerosene lantern, kerosene stove and kerosene refrigerator filled the space. But there was no kerosene.

My thoughts returned to the PCVs and what they might have done. I envisioned the refrigerator running and full of cold beer. Then I just envisioned the beer. It didn't have to be cold, just plentiful. But there wasn't any beer, there wasn't any light, there wasn't any drinkable water and there wasn't any food. It promised to be a long night.

"I need to visit the outhouse," Jo Ann announced. My bladder gave an empathetic twinge. Our last pee stop had been in Monrovia. The three of us trooped outside. Jo took the flashlight and disappeared into the rickety one holer.

"Curtis!" she yelled. I yanked open the door and prepared to be heroic. Jo Ann was standing inside with a wild look on her face. The flashlight was shining down into the hole. Thousands of little eyes stared back at us.

"Lots of cockroaches," Sam noted. He was beginning to sound repetitious.

That was the night that Jo Ann mastered her famous levitating squat routine. Cockroaches used your butt as a runway when you sat on the toilet. Jo solved the problem by positioning herself about five inches up in the air. I am not sure how she managed this Yoga feat but her rear never touched an outhouse seat during the two years we were in Africa. I used a different approach. A loud stomp on the floor sent the cockroaches scurrying downward. The trick was to escape before they climbed back to the top. My habit of reading in the bathroom was sacrificed to the cause.

There wasn't much left to do but send Sam on his way and try to get some sleep. We retired to our bedroom, and I scrutinized the walls to see if any new monster crab spiders had reappeared. They hadn't. Word of their truncated life span had gotten around.

I then beat the bed for several minutes with the sincere hope of persuading any other unwanted guests to hit the road.

I also leaned the rest of our furniture, three well-used Salvation Army type folding chairs, against each of our three screened windows. Veteran Peace Corps Volunteers had warned us that rogues, i.e. burglars, loved to rob green Volunteers on their first few days in town. The chairs would serve as a primitive burglar alarm. My theory was that jiggling the window would knock over the chair and scare away the rogue. It was guaranteed to scare the hell out of us.

Finally it was time to crawl in. We left our clothes on. Jo Ann, by this point, had reached such a high level of unhappiness, I was glad there were no handy airplanes around to cart her home. There was a story about a Volunteer who had landed at Robert's Field Airport, taken one look around, and climbed back on the plane. My perspective on the evening was that things had been bad enough, they were bound to get better.

That's when the drums and screaming started.

No one had told us that a Kpelle funeral was like an Irish wake. Mourners stayed up all night pounding on drums, wailing, and drinking lots of cane juice, a concoction similar in nature to moonshine. It was important that the dead be sent off properly. Otherwise, the spirit of the dead person would become irritated, hang around, and do all sorts of bad stuff.

Of course we knew nothing about any of this. All we knew was that people were beating on drums and screaming. It was time to circle the wagons. Eventually, I went to sleep; I don't think Jo ever did.

CHAPTER 14

CRAZY FLUMO SHAKES MY HAND—AND ANKLES

A new day did manage to happen, as they always do. Jo Ann and I promised to make it a good one. Her job was to mount a ferocious counter offensive on the bug-a-bugs and cockroaches. Sam was coming early with a broom. My job was to walk the quarter mile to town, buy five gallons of kerosene, find the most toxic bug spray known to humankind and scavenge anything available that resembled food.

I added alcohol to the list.

But first I needed to replace the malarial pond residing in our front room. I grabbed the offending bucket and tossed the stagnant water onto a plant. "Waste not; want not," my mother would have urged even though it was in the middle of Liberia's rainy season and the plant had already received half of its annual 170 inches of rain.

Now I was ready to tackle the well. My family had one when I was growing up. It came with a cover, a high-pitched whirring pump, and a holding tank. Except for power outages, we could depend on it to magically deliver water day in and day out.

Our well in Gbarnga was an unprotected hole in the ground waiting for someone to fall in. In the US, I would have been sued if someone came within 50 feet of it. Next to the well I found a frayed rope. I tied it to the bucket's handle using a Boy Scout bowline. Then, making sure I had a firm hold on the end of the rope, I tossed the bucket into the dark hole.

Kersplash! I gave it a shake so it would tip over and fill. A five-gallon bucket of water weighs 43 pounds. By the time I yanked it over the edge, I had a new appreciation for modern technology— and for the Volunteer who had left the original bucket in our house.

I delivered my burden to Jo and started for town. Half of Gbarnga was standing along the road staring at me. I smiled and waved a lot, like a princess on parade. They smiled and waved back.

Soon I came to the town's main street. Open-air shops lined the dirt road on both sides. At first, they looked the same: white washed walls, rusted zinc roofs and dark interiors. Shadowy faces stared out from inside. Then I began noticing differences. Several were fronted with crumbling cement steps that had long since given up any hope of connecting to the eroded street. One featured a crocodile skin nailed to the front post, its tail dragging in the dirt. Another had brightly colored shirts and shorts strung up like Christmas ornaments.

Two or three were obviously makeshift bars, no more than holes in the wall with people bellying up to planks. An ancient Liberian 'Ma' came staggering out of one with a half-pint bottle of gin clutched in her hand. She noticed me, hoisted her bottle in a toast, and took a swig.

A few shops were larger and resembled country stores filled with the minutia of daily life. Pale-faced Lebanese leased the shops. Lebanese made up the majority of Liberia's middle class but were not allowed to own property. I was headed for a shop that Sam had recommended.

A group of men stood idly in front of the store. Had folks known I was coming, I would have sworn it was a reception committee. *It's show time* went reverberating around my skull. I put on my best Peace Corps smile. One of the men stepped forward to greet me. He was barefoot and wore a tattered shirt, tattered shorts and a big grin. His hand shot out.

This is it, I thought, my first official Liberian handshake. We had started practicing in San Francisco. The shake begins as a normal handshake but ends with you snapping each other's fingers. An audible snap signifies success. It isn't easy at first. If the person is really happy to see you, he may go through the process two or three times.

(About the time the snap becomes second nature, it's time to go home. Then you have to unlearn the process. Your American friends look at you strangely when you snap their fingers. At least my conservative Republican father-in-law did. But back to Africa.)

We shook; our hands parted. *Snap!* It worked. All of the men beamed and I beamed back. Their official greeter grabbed my hand again. Snap! Another success and more beaming. And again. Then a fourth time. Nobody had mentioned four times to me and this time the guy wouldn't let go. The men were laughing out loud now.

My hundred-watt smile became a twenty-watt grimace as I politely tried to retrieve my hand. No luck. I steeled myself, gave up any pretense of being polite and yanked. My hand pulled free and I breathed a huge sigh of relief. It lasted as long as it took the guy to drop to the ground and wrap his arms around my ankles. By now the other men were all but rolling the street.

I had become prime time entertainment, the George Custer of Gbarnga. I might still be there if the cavalry hadn't arrived. It came in the form of a handsome Liberian man in a well-tailored suit. He appeared on the scene and gave Flumo a healthy kick in the butt. Flumo let go.

"Hi, I am Daniel Goe, Vice Principal at Gboveh High School. Welcome to Gbarnga." he introduced himself.

We shook hands in the old fashioned way as Daniel explained that the man who had his arms wrapped around me was known throughout the Country as Crazy Flumo. I wasn't the only person to receive his attention. Once, Daniel told me, Flumo had thrown himself down in front of Vice President Tolbert's car and wouldn't move until the VP climbed out and gave him five dollars.

I later learned that a tall Texan Peace Corps Volunteer had walked several yards down the main street of Gbarnga with Flumo tenaciously attached to one leg. I'd gotten off easy. Having met one of Gbarnga's true characters, I was about to meet another.

CHAPTER 15

MY NAME IS CAPTAIN DIE

Fortunately, my adventures for the day were over. I bought kerosene, found a bug poison so potent it was outlawed it in the US, and discovered fine culinary treats including canned beef from Argentina and Club Beer, the national brew. The canned beef and beer would become staples in our diet.

Jo Ann and Sam beat back the bug-a-bug and arrived at an uneasy truce with the cockroaches. The latter would limit their forays until after we had gone to bed, and stay out of our bedroom. In return, we would only kill those cockroaches we could reasonably stomp without tearing our house down. For a while, I maintained a squashed cockroach account on a paper that I taped to the door. Somewhere around 70, I gave up.

I have a grudging respect for cockroaches; they have a bit of seniority over man, some 300 million years worth. Back before dinosaurs roamed the earth, cockroaches were hiding out in all of the nooks and crannies. Their six legged progeny will probably be around long after humankind has gone the way of the big 'lizards.' There are reportedly somewhere between 3500 and 4000 species crawling around, and each species has a shot at survival. Compare that with our odds. Anyway, there we were, one happy little family, cockroaches and all. Jo and I were about to begin our career as elementary school teachers. But we had another adventure before facing our first class; Captain Die appeared on our doorstep.

He was a well digger who was said to have spent too much time in dark holes. He had dug the well that came with our house for the two female Peace Corps Volunteers we replaced. Afterwards, he began stopping by to visit the women and bum cigarettes. They had been quite accommodating; he expected the same service from us.

"Bock, bock," we heard on our third day in town as Jo and I prepared for lunch. Liberian's tended to verbalize their knocking and "bock, bock" was good Liberian English for "knock, knock." I went to the door and was treated to a unique introduction.

"Hello, my name is Captain Die. My name is Captain Die because I am going to die some day. This is my dog, Rover. Roll over Rover. Give me a cigarette." Rover, who was a big ugly dog of indeterminate parenthood, dutifully rolled over. It made quite an impression.

We explained to Captain Die that neither of us smoked. As a substitute, we invited him in to share some ice tea Jo had just brewed. We gave the Captain a glass and he took a huge swallow. I have no idea what he thought he was getting, but it wasn't Lipton's. It seems he thought we were trying to poison him. A look of terror crossed his face and he spat the ice tea out in a forceful spray that covered half the kitchen and us. Dripping wet, we found ourselves caught between concern, laughter and dismay. The Captain marched out of our house in disgust with Rover close behind.

In addition to having found our predecessors to be an excellent supply of tobacco, Captain Die was quite taken with one of them. While the story may have been apocryphal, we were told he appeared at the door when Maryanne's parents were visiting from the States. Captain Die was a man on a mission. He was going to request Maryanne's hand in marriage.

I've always imagined the scene this way. Maryanne's parents are sitting in the living room on the Salvation Army chairs, making a game attempt at hiding their culture shock when this big black man and his ugly dog appear at the screen door. Maryanne jumps up and says, "Oh, Mom and Dad, I would like you to meet my friend, Captain Die." Mom and Dad, brainwashed by Emily Post, and wishing to appear nonchalant, quickly stand up with strained smiles on their faces.

Captain Die grabs Dad's hand and tries to snap his finger at the same time proclaiming, "Hello, my name is Captain Die. My name is Captain Die because I am going to die some day. This is my dog Rover. Roll over Rover. Give me your daughter."

No one told me how Maryanne's parents responded to the good Captain's offer so I will leave the ending up to the reader's imagination. I can report that Maryanne was not whisked out of the country by her mom and dad.

In addition to the certifiable types who found PCVs an easy target for their weirdness, there were a lot of folks who were just plain curious about how we lived. One little girl would have put a cat to shame. I never could figure out where she came from. She would stand on our porch with her nose pressed against the screen door and stare at us for what seemed like hours. After a while, it would become disconcerting, and I'd suggest she go home. She would disappear but then I'd look up and there she'd be again, little nose pressed flat.

After our initial experience of moving in, fighting with bugs, and meeting Crazy Flumo and Captain Die, it seemed like teaching would be easy. It wasn't.

CHAPTER 16

GOOD MORNING TEACHA

I put on my coat and tie and shined my shoes. Jo donned her best dress. Kids were streaming by our house and staring through the screens, hoping for a glance at the new teachers. Jo and I smiled at each other, took a deep breath and walked out the door.

The air was warm and thick with humidity. Towering cumulus clouds filled the sky. Distant thunder rumbled. Rain was coming. We turned left on the red dirt road and joined the parade of students who glanced shyly at us. Massaquoi Elementary School waited. It wasn't far, a half mile at most, just far enough to get sweaty. Lush growth lined the road. Green, dense and impenetrable, it was alive with biting insects and slithering snakes. The school sat off to the right in a clearing that been hacked out of the jungle.

Four classrooms faced the road. Two more, placed on the ends, faced inward and formed an elongated U. Cement blocks painted blue sat on top of cement blocks painted brown. Palm trees peeked over the zinc roof. Shuttered windows and closed doors completed the simple structure. A flagpole with Liberia's fluttering red, white and blue flag was planted exactly in the center of the yard.

Students and teachers milled about as we approached. All eyes were on us, two white people in a sea of black. A man broke free from the crowd and approached. It was the principal. We smiled and shook hands and he pointed out our classrooms. That was it; the orientation was over. And so was the gathering. Students and teachers moved toward their rooms. Jo Ann wished me good luck and stalked off to her first grade with a look of determination. I walked toward my second grade with a look of bemusement.

"Good Morning Teacha!" thirty bright and shiny faces shouted in unison as I entered.

It was scary— scarier than the big burly policeman who had guarded the door to the administration building at Berkeley. I was expected to entertain and actually teach these kids something over the next couple of years. "How?" bounced around in my skull and jumped down to my stomach.

I had had a total of two months training at San Francisco State University on educational theory. I didn't have a clue about managing a classroom of second graders or teaching reading and writing and arithmetic. The last time I had been in a second grade, I was seven years old. My four-week stint as a student teacher might be helpful. But how would teaching a classroom of middle-class kids in South San Francisco, California relate to teaching a classroom of tribal Africans in Gbarnga, Liberia?

These students came from another world: a world where spirits lived in trees, ghosts were dangerous, chicken guts foretold the future, termites were considered a delicacy, and tribal justice was determined with a red-hot machete.

"Good morning students," I replied and smiled. Look confidant, I urged myself. Take control. It became my mantra.

I walked up to the blackboard and wrote *Mr. Mekemson.* The silence of the room was broken by the squeakiness of the chalk. I introduced myself, pronounced my name and had them pronounce it— several times. They laughed.

"I am from California," I explained and noticed a slight recognition. Hollywood was there. "It's a long way off." I sketched a map of North America, Africa and the Atlantic Ocean with X's for California and Liberia. Then I drew a great circle route with Diamond Springs on one end and

Gbarnga on the other. I added a large jet plane with me looking out the window.

It was my first geography lesson. Of course it was incomprehensible. The kids had never seen a map. The only distance they understood was one they could walk. Jet airplanes were rare tiny specks in the sky. But they liked the picture of me looking out the airplane window.

"OK, it's your turn. I want you to tell me your name, your age and what tribe you belong to." I imagined Americo-Liberians in Monrovia frowning at the tribal question. We were supposed to encourage our students to think of themselves as Liberians as opposed to being Kpelle or Mano or Bassa or any one of several other ethnic groups they belonged to. While I understood and agreed with the government's objective, the students weren't there yet. They were still tribal first and Liberian second, a distant second.

The majority of my students were Kpelle. It was the largest tribe in Liberia and Gbarnga was in the heart of Kpelle country. But there were also several other ethnic groups. English was the common language that was supposed to bind them together. Tribal dialects were not allowed in the classroom. I quickly learned that *English* meant Pidgin English spoken with a deep Liberian accent. At first, it seemed like a foreign language.

For example, Jo Ann might say to me, "I have to go down town for about twenty minutes. I promise I won't be gone long. Please wait for me." My students would say, "Wait small, I go come." To make things even more confusing to an American, "small" could mean a few hours.

One idiom I learned quickly was, "Teacha, I have to serve nature." That meant, "May I have your permission to use the restroom?" Actually it was permission to use the outhouse, or just as likely the jungle, or even the side of the building. One day I looked up and saw one of my male students standing outside and listening to me through the window. I saw a slight shake of his shoulder and realized he was peeing on the wall. I admired his dedication but discouraged the practice.

Another challenge I faced was age difference. My youngest second-grade student was a decent second-grade age of seven. The oldest was 22, my age, and a heck of a lot tougher. Several were middle-school age and had middle-school attitudes.

Books created a different problem; for the most part, there weren't any. What we had for reading were vintage 1950 California readers complete with Dick, Jane and Spot. I suspect I should have been grateful for anything, but it was difficult for tribal kids to identify with big white houses, white picket fences and little white kids. As for Spot, he bore a striking resemblance to food. Later, when I had a cat, my students would stop by and tease me by pinching him and saying, "Oh, Mr. Mekemson, what sweet meat-o."

My room reflected the simplicity of the building. Shutters covered windows without glass and without screens. Open shutters provided air conditioning. Bugs were free to come and go. Closed shutters kept heat in and tropical deluges out. The only audio-visual aid available was my writing on the blackboard.

Eventually we got through introductions, seat assignments and the other chores inherent during the first day of class. It was time to teach. I broke out Dick, Jane and Spot.

Somehow I managed to struggle through that first day. It helped that there was a curriculum to follow and that the two experienced Peace Corps teachers we replaced had taught the kids basic skills such as sitting in their seats, being relatively quiet, and raising their hands.

Back home after school, Jo had a story to tell.

"I was reading the *Owl and the Pussy Cat* out loud when one of my first graders broke in and said, 'Oh, Mrs. Mekemson, you shouldn't say that!' The whole class broke out in laughter. I asked them what they were talking about. They clammed up. All I could get was nervous giggles. After school I related the story to one of the Liberian teachers and asked if she had any idea what the kids were talking about. She clammed up as well but I pushed her."

"You were reading about a pussy, Mrs. Mekemson," the woman managed to stutter. "You know, a woman's down-under."

How in the world had her first graders, who could barely speak English, picked up this particular meaning of pussy? We didn't have a clue.

CHAPTER 17

"YOU ARE LATE, MRS. TUBMAN."

Our life became routine, if living without electricity or running water and parking your butt in a cockroach occupied outhouse can be considered routine.

Morning started with a quick bowl of cereal topped off by a mixture of water and Milkman powder. Liking powdered milk involved developing an acquired taste that I never acquired, but fresh milk came with a question mark. Louis Pasteur had not made it to Gbarnga. Tuberculosis could exist in raw milk.

Water was equally scary. Amoebic dysentery is a common third-world ailment that attacks your intestines. Innards react with shock and awe; think of it as Montezuma's Revenge times ten. The Peace Corps provided a ceramic filter, and the Peace Corps doctor provided endless warnings. Paranoia ran rampant in our household. We boiled our water for ten minutes and then filtered it, even when it came straight from the rain barrel.

By 8:00 our screen door slammed behind us as we made our daily trek to Massaquoi and teaching. At least I hoped that was what I was doing. Nobody nominated me for teacher of the year but I was feeling less nervous about the job. In Peace Corps, you take your victories where you find them. I liked my students and followed the curriculum. Showing enthusiasm for the subject matter was more difficult.

"Here comes Jane. She looks mad. Run Dick run," did not get me excited. Neither did two plus three equals five or "Let's see if you can print an A."

While I felt challenged as a teacher, I had advantages the Liberian teachers didn't. Most were getting by with a high school education. Pay was $40 per month without benefits. Adding injury to insult, they were required to 'contribute' one month of their annual salary to the True Whig Party. In fact, loyalty to the Party was often how you got your job.

Between taking care of their families and illness, teachers were often absent. Sadly, no teacher meant no teaching. Substitutes were nonexistent. The kids were left to get by on their own, which they did like kids everywhere— laughing, yelling, fighting, playing games, and disrupting other classrooms. Sometimes, out of frustration, I would walk into an unsupervised classroom and be rewarded with instant silence. It lasted until I walked out the door.

Occasionally, we escaped from our jobs. The students would be called out to join a work party, there would be a national holiday, or an important politician would come to town.

Work parties involved beating the jungle back from the school. Vine-covered trees lurked around the edges, eager to regain lost territory. All of the students were required to participate in chopping and hauling. We were expected to supervise. The older boys wielded machetes.

My 22-year old second grader, John, challenged me to a tree-cutting contest. It was a small tree, limb size. Naturally the whole class and half the school gathered around. I good-naturedly took the machete, sent a prayer to the forest spirits that I wouldn't chop off my leg, and whacked downward with all my strength. The machete bit 'small' into the sapling, maybe an inch, and became stuck, super glued to the tree. The kids broke out in laughter, very loud laughter.

"Your turn," I said to John, leaving the offending tool buried. He grabbed the handle, yanked the blade out, and swung the machete in one easy motion. The tree came crashing down. I told John he was now in charge of class discipline. The kids laughed again, but not so hard. Maybe I was serious.

Holidays normally celebrated some important event in Americo-Liberian history, like Matilda Newport Day. Matilda had saved the fledgling colony of freed slaves from America by using a canon to mow down the tribal Liberians who were attacking in an effort to regain their land. Even though the battle had taken place over 100 years earlier, tribal people were still miffed that they were expected to celebrate the event. We sympathized but appreciated the day off.

When President Tubman or Vice President Tolbert came to town, school children were expected to line the streets and cheer. It was part of the National Unification Program. Tubman was the charismatic 'father' of his nation, the big daddy. Teachers were expected to be there as well. And they were. It's not smart to irritate your meal ticket.

Our presence was urged but not required. Most Volunteers opted out of the important-politician-parade, mainly because politicians were never on time. Often the luminary was two or three hours late, and it was pouring down rain, which it did half of the time, or the sun was boiling hot, which it did the other half.

One of our fellow Peace Corps teachers in Gbarnga, Phil Weisberg, took a different approach. He was a tall, gangly Volunteer who looked like he had recently lost something of profound value. He rarely laughed.

I remember three other things about him. One, he was in love with Barbara Streisand. He had all of her albums and would listen to her for hours on his battery-driven record player. Two, he instituted his own welfare system for needy Liberian kids. He would hire one kid to dig a hole in his backyard and a second to fill it in. Sam thought this was quite funny and laughed when he told us the story. Three, if his students had to wait in the sun or rain for politicians, he was going to be there, suffering along with them.

Once, when he was waiting in the hot sun for the President's wife, Phil decided to demonstrate his displeasure. He penned a sign that informed Mrs. Tubman, "You are late." Two hours later her motorcade tooled in to Gbarnga. Phil hoisted his sign and waved it at the First Lady's limousine.

The protest lived only as long as it took the security police to grab him. One didn't mess with the President's wife. One did not protest against the government. After Phil had had sufficient time to consider his crime, Mrs. Tubman directed the police to release him. For punishment, he was transferred to Monrovia to teach Americo-Liberian children at a Methodist school. Eventually, he returned to his teaching job in Gbarnga.

When Phil's term expired, he left his record player and collection with us, minus Barbara. It did include a great selection of the Kingston Trio songs, however. Sam spent his spare time getting *Charlie off the MTA* and *Tom Dooley hung*.

CHAPTER 18

A QUIVERING CARCASS

Our morning routine was followed by our afternoon routine. We finished each day of teaching by 1:00 p.m. and assigned it to the done pile. Our standard reward for our morning's work was a PB&J sandwich washed down by orange Kool-Aid. Sam joined us. We bought the jelly and peanut butter from the Lebanese market. The bread came from the local baker where the glass display case had more flies on the inside than the outside. Sometimes, the bread included bug parts. We looked before we bit.

Naptime was next; I fell in love with siestas. Rainy season helped. Torrential afternoon showers pounded down on our zinc roof, cooled the air, and lulled us to sleep. An hour later we rolled off the bed and jumped into lesson planning.

Monday through Friday, Sam cooked Liberian chop for the three of us. On Saturdays, Jo cooked Kwi food (western food) for him, usually pasta of some type. He had a teenager's appetite and our budget was tight. On Sundays, Sam was off.

Chop consisted of a thick soup made up of meat, greens, hot peppers, bouillon, tomato paste and palm oil. It was served on top of country rice, the staple crop and food of the Kpelle. The rice was raised on the hillsides rather than in swamps and arrived with small stones that Sam carefully picked out. Biting down on a rock might warrant a trip to the dentist and the nearest one was in Monrovia. In addition to the inconvenience of the trip, the dentist was likely to find 15 cavities you didn't have. Peace Corps paid well.

Most of our ingredients for chop came from Gbarnga's thriving open-air market, but not the meat. A 6:00 a.m. Saturday trip to the market to buy fresh beef convinced us that canned beef from Argentina was really delicious. The butcher carved our order for steak off a still-quivering carcass that had been a live steer an hour earlier. Steak, we learned, was anything without bone. And it was not marbled in fat. Forget corn fed. Liberian cattle were rib-showing skinny and fed off of any grass they could hustle. Their meat was as tough as they were. We sacrificed our purchase to an old-fashioned meat grinder and cooked it to death. After that, obtaining meat involved making a trip to the Lebanese market and opening a can.

The market was great for greens. Collards, eggplants, pumpkins, potato greens and bitter balls were all options. Collard and potato greens were my favorites. Bitter balls tasted exactly like their name— eating them one time was once too many. The number of peppers thrown in depended on tolerance for hot. We progressed from being one-pepper-people to three-pepper-people during our stay. Palm oil added a unique, almost nutty taste.

The market was filled with tribal women selling everything from palm oil to large snails that constantly escaped from their tubs and crawled off. 'Small boys' were sent to retrieve them. Sam refused to cook the fist-size gastropods. "They are taboo for my family." Taboo was a word he had learned from an anthropologist. I wasn't sure about the taboo part but hung in with him on his refusal to cook snails. I had no more desire for dining on the slimy creatures than he did.

Produce was carried to market in large metal bowls that the women balanced on their heads with ramrod-straight backs and ballerina grace. Given enough beer, I wandered around our house trying to master the skill of head loading. My record was five seconds before everything came crashing down.

The women wore brightly colored *lappas* (wrap around skirts) with blouses and headscarves. They would squat next to their produce and call out prices. Large, juicy oranges were "one cent, one cent" in season. Grapefruits were "five cent, five cent" and giant pineapples a quarter. Avocados, or butter pears, as the Liberians called them, could also be purchased for a few cents.

The oranges sported green skins and the pineapples, ant nests, but both were 'sweet-o.' We added orange juice to our orange Kool-Aid. Plopping the pineapples into a bucket of water overnight did in the ants. By morning they were little black floaters, forming a scum on top of the water.

Our appearance at the market caused inflation but bargaining was expected. We took along Sam whose rapid Kpelle ensured that everyone received a fair deal. Eventually Sam took over the shopping chores. We'd send him off with five dollars and he would bring home a week's worth of food.

When dark arrived in its efficient tropical fashion, we would light our kerosene lantern and get cozy. Peace Corps supplied each Volunteer with a book locker filled with one hundred books. We considered it our responsibility to read them all. TV was not an option. I was curious about who made the book selections. My money was on a Harvard professor of literature. The book lockers were heavy on classics and short on mysteries and sci-fi.

Occasionally, we would add a game of scrabble or cards to our evening routine. Around 10:00 p.m., it was time for us to eliminate any cockroaches that had strayed into our bedroom and drift off to dreamland.

CHAPTER 19

A SHORT LESSON ON CATS AND GUACAMOLE

The American anthropologist James Gibbs is one of the world's leading experts on the Kpelle culture. As it turns out, he was living in Gbarnga when we arrived and Sam was working for him as an informant on Kpelle customs. During this experience, Sam had learned the word *taboo* he liberally applied to the snails he didn't want to eat.

One evening, James and his wife Jewelle invited Jo Ann and me over for dinner. It was our first invitation out as Peace Corps Volunteers. We were pleased but nervous. Being recent college graduates, we were still awed by academicians. We dressed up in our best clothes and headed down the road past Massaquoi School to their house.

The Gibbs had an impressive house for upcountry Liberia. They were sophisticated, nice folks who quickly put us at ease. Among the hors d'oeuvres was a concoction of mashed avocado, tomatoes and peppers that Jo and I found quite tasteful. We made the mistake of asking what it was.

"Why it's guacamole of course," Dr. Gibbs declared. We must have looked blank because he went on, "Surely anyone from California knows what guacamole is."

Surely we didn't. I felt like Barbara Streisand in *Funny Girl* when she learned that pate was mashed chicken liver. It was 1965, and Mexican food had yet to storm Northern California. Yes, we'd been to UC Berkeley, but dining out in Berkeley on a survival budget had meant beer and pizza at La Val's or a greasy hamburger at Kip's. To change the subject, I called attention to their cat.

"Nice cat," I noted.

Mrs. Gibbs gushed. "She's in love."

Dr. Gibbs jumped in, obviously glad to leave the subject of guacamole. "The boys are coming by every night to visit. We hear them yowl their affection up on the roof."

The cat looked quite proud of her accomplishments. Having been properly introduced, she strolled over and rubbed up against my legs. I reached down and scratched her head, which served as an invitation to climb into my lap. While arranging herself she provided me with a tails-eye view. Staring back at me was the anatomy of the most impressive tomcat I've ever seen.

I could hardly contain myself. "Um, she isn't a she," I managed to get out while struggling to maintain a straight face.

"What do you mean?" Dr. Gibbs asked in his best professorial voice. Rather than respond verbally, I turned the cat around and aimed his tail at Dr. Gibbs. Understanding flitted across his face.

"We never thought to look," he mumbled lamely. We were even. While the country kids from the hills might not know their guacamole from mashed avocados, they did know basic anatomy.

CHAPTER 20

DIRT ROADS DON'T HAVE WHITE LINES

When we boarded the Pan Am jet at JFK, we abandoned the life we had known. Three-inch cockroaches, a rickety outhouse, and a hole-in-the-ground well came with the territory, as did boiling our water, reading by lantern, and eating chop. For the most part, we had adapted well.

We had kids to teach, collard greens to eat, and a zinc roof to keep out the rain. Serving as a married couple, we also had each other— our own little society. Plus we had Sam. He was bright, funny, and provided an introduction to the Kpelle culture. He also did many of the chores.

Life was almost too easy, too routine. We were good at entertaining ourselves, a fundamental skill for Peace Corps Volunteers, but we had jumped from racing down a multi-lane freeway to walking on a dirt path. The tumultuous year at Berkeley, marriage, Peace Corps training and Africa had happened bang, bang, bang. Now life was more like drip, drip, drip.

After two months we were climbing the walls like bug-a-bug. We needed a break. Relief came in the form of an invitation from our friend Morris Carpenter. He had escaped from Yopea and landed a job teaching sixth-graders in Ganta, 30 miles upcountry from us. Wellington Sirleaf, the Peace Corps driver, dropped off the note. Since there was neither phone nor mail service, Wellington was our once-a-week contact with the outside world.

I found it amusing that Morris and I lived closer together in Liberia than we had in California. Getting from Gbarnga to Ganta, however, was more challenging than getting from Diamond Springs to Auburn. We had two options: money bus or taxi.

The money bus was the more colorful choice. Think of taking a UPS cargo van, cutting out windows, attaching a roof rack, and cramming it full of people, pigs, chickens, goats, bags of rice, fresh produce, luggage boxes and anything else a Liberian might need to survive on or sell.

These workhorses of the Liberian transportation system disdained schedules and stopped frequently. Minimal shocks, uncovered wood benches and bumpy dirt roads guaranteed that butts were begging for mercy inside of thirty minutes. Packed conditions denied wiggle room to relieve an aching tailbone, but might provide a kid or rooster for your lap. And there was always a chance of a breakdown accompanied by the fervent hope that your driver would fix the problem in under three hours.

We decided that our daily life provided enough cross-cultural adventure and opted for the taxi. We packed a bag, left Sam in charge of buying a chicken, and walked into town to where the taxis gathered. A dirty, grey, battered Peugeot was leaving for Ganta in a short time. "Ten dolla," the driver informed us. "Five dolla," we countered. Seven was the agreed price for the two of us. Then it was time to 'wait small.' The driver wanted more passengers. After about an hour he gave up.

Any thoughts of a civilized trip in to Ganta were dispelled in the first five minutes. The driver drove as if he saw a green mamba in his rearview mirror and the snake was gaining. While the law required us to be on the right side, dirt roads don't have white lines. I doubt it mattered. When a car-eating pothole was located on our side of the road, we were on the other, even on a blind curve. It wasn't a game of chicken; it was Russian roulette. Occasionally the driver would honk his horn.

Fortunately, the ride was relatively short. Our introduction to Ganta was a road barrier backed up by an armed soldier.

"You pay," the driver informed us. He had neglected to tell us there was a fee for entering the town. Turns out it was a bribe, or a dash as they call it in West Africa. "Five dolla," the soldier demanded as he looked at us menacingly. It made me angry but I took out two dollars and handed them to the driver. "Five dolla," the soldier repeated. I shook my head no. The soldier glared at me again and then took the proffered money. Ever so slowly he opened the gate. Bribes were a way of life in Liberia as they are in much of the world. It was a game we had to play, but we didn't have to like it. "Asshole," I mumbled as we drove off.

Ganta's taxi stand included a mini-mart. Tribal women were sitting on the ground and selling everything from pineapples to palm nuts. One woman, wearing a black-and-white-wrap-around lappa, featured five metal basins filled with what appeared to be smoked animal parts. I looked more closely. A small, shrunken-head sized skull glared up at me with vacant eyes. A dozen or so other skulls looked elsewhere. Another basin contained legs, another split rib cages, and another long, curved tails. It was monkey meat.

"You buy?" the woman asked. "No thank you," I replied a bit to hastily. Monkey was not on my list of preferred foods. She laughed.

A small boy appeared in front of me and shoved a boiled egg in my face. "Ten cents," he demanded.

"I will give you ten cents to take us to Teacha Carpenter's house," I countered.

"Twenty." "Fifteen." "Okay." We had struck a bargain.

Teacha Carpenter was waiting for us with a cold beer and laughed at our stories. He was a veteran PCV at the end of his term. We were green Volunteers at the beginning. Our traumas were everyday life to him. He had his own tales. An army of mice lived in his attic.

"I hear them doing parade drills every night. Back and forth, back and forth with the sergeant barking orders." He had hired Metternich the Cat to solve the problem. Each morning Metternich deposited two or three dead rodents for inspection. He was making a significant reduction in the mouse population. Besides all the mice he could eat, Metternich took his pay in chop.

Morris had planned a tour of the local leper colony for us. In particular, he wanted us to meet Freddie, a wood-carver he had befriended. Leprosy, Morris explained as we walked over to the colony, is hard to catch. We were glad to hear there was little danger, but still wary. Most of what we knew about the disease related to the old horror stories, the ones that led communities to ban lepers to remote locations. Losing body parts is scary. While leprosy might not be highly contagious, it was still contagious.

A neat row of cabins surrounded by banana, avocado and palm trees greeted us. It seemed that the lepers were well cared for and well fed. Freddie reinforced my opinion. He had a lean-to studio and was dressed in a clean white T-shirt, jeans and polished brown shoes. Chips were flying as he chopped away on a block with a curved-head adze. The smell of freshly cut wood permeated the air. A scroungy brown and white dog was lying off to the side. It opened an eye, gave a partial wag, and went back to sleep.

I couldn't stop myself from checking to see if Freddie had lost any limbs. Except for grey blotches on his hands, he appeared intact. A devil mask was displayed beside him. Other carvings were stacked against the wall. Freddie grinned as we admired his carvings. It was obvious that he took pride in his work, that he had found a way to soften the fright his disease must cause.

I was developing a taste for African art. Its primitive subject matter jumped past my rational mind and captured my subconscious. I found one piece particularly appealing. Two large feet were connected to stumpy legs that disappeared into a shapeless robe that flared downward from the neck. There were no arms. A gigantic head with a mouthful of 28 teeth and a large nose topped off the neck. It was like a circus clown, both scary and humorous.

"It's a Bush Devil," Morris explained. The Bush Devil, so named by disapproving missionaries, was a powerful force within the tribal society. I happily broke out five dollars and bought the piece.

Back at Morris's we ate four-pepper chop, drank more beer, told more tales and went to sleep with mice marching back and forth in the attic.

CHAPTER 21

GETTING A-HEAD IN KAKATA

Food popped into my mind on the taxi trip home from Ganta. After two months of eating Argentina's finest canned beef, I had found myself lusting after the neighbor's chickens. My last instructions to Sam before leaving to visit Morris had been to buy us one for the stew pot. I had visions of arriving back home with the hen waiting for us in the refrigerator, ready to be cooked. It was a pleasant, if short-lived, dream.

The chicken was roosting on our stove and appeared to like her new home. Generous piles of chicken poop decorated the kitchen. Sam and I had discussed my preferences before we left. Apparently the instructions had not been clear. I corrected the error.

"Here's another dollar. Take this chicken out and have her killed, gutted and plucked."

My chicken whacking days from Peace Corps training were over. Sam returned a couple of hours later with dinner and Jo Ann did her culinary thing. The final product met all of my mouth-watering expectations. When the bones had been picked clean I worked my way through the pile again. Chicken had never tasted better, before or since. But there was a close match.

"Chicken and rice with palm butter is nice," the lyrics to a popular West African tune proclaimed. I agreed; it was my favorite chop. Palm butter has a unique sweet flavor and rich texture. Unfortunately, pounding palm nuts was clearly defined as women's work, which Sam avoided with passion. A stonewall divided male and female roles within the Kpelle culture. Only when I had threatened to trade him in on a house girl to get palm butter did Sam miraculously find a way to obtain the illusive product.

It was possible to eat well in Gbarnga, even on our $160 per month salaries. But there were times we longed for a convenient grocery store packed with rib eye steaks, fresh milk and ice cream. Or, even better, a restaurant where we could order such food. The visit with Morris had provided a break in our routine, but Morris lived the same way we did. His chop was quite tasty, but it was still chop. Jo and I decided it was time for our first trip back to Monrovia. Once again we packed our bags and headed over to Gbarnga's taxi stand.

This time the price was $15 for the two of us. The taxi was packed and I rode shotgun. My job was to put my thumb on the windshield whenever we met another vehicle. The theory was that this would keep the windshield from imploding if struck by a rock. Shatterproof glass hadn't made it to Liberia.

Rainforest, villages and small towns whizzed by slowly. I felt like we were caught in a time warp. An occasional burned out hulk of a money bus or taxi decorated the roadside and reminded us of our mortality. We passed Phebe Hospital built and operated by Lutheran missionaries, and then Cuttington College built and operated by Episcopal missionaries.

Tribal Liberians waited with Zen-like patience beside the road for their unscheduled money bus rides. Usually a faint trail led off into the bush to their villages. I wondered what they thought about while waiting. Did they ponder their reception in Monrovia as they descended on relatives who lived in tin shacks already overflowing with people?

In the town of Suakoko, we dropped one passenger and picked up another. He was chewing on a dark, smoky leg of either dog or monkey meat. My stomach growled in appreciation. I was adjusting to Africa.

At some point, the jungle gave way to rubber trees with bark slashed to drain the white sticky substance. We had entered the world's largest rubber tree plantation. Owned by Firestone, it was known for the low wages it paid Liberian workers and the generous payoffs it made to government officials.

With Kakata came relief, a paved road. Several America-Liberians had large farms in the area. Their names were a who's who of Liberia's elite. Morris had reveled in telling us a story about a scandalous murder that had happened in the town. The guy's body had been dismembered. His head ended up in a toilet. The local Peace Corps Volunteer told anyone who would listen, "If you want to get a-head in life, come to Kakata."

Eventually we made it to Monrovia and our taxi let us off at the Peace Corps hostel. I'd be bunking with the guys and Jo Ann would be bunking with the girls. I didn't think much of sleeping with a group of snoring men but the price was right. Plus Abijoudi's was waiting.

Abijoudi's was a genuine supermarket; it was close to heaven. I am not sure what was more impressive: the air conditioning or the aisles crammed with goods. We wandered awestruck up and down the rows staring at the canned and frozen foods from around the world. And then we splurged. Jo Ann bought a frozen duck from Holland. Morris was coming to Gbarnga for a return visit. It would be the first meal she had ever cooked for a guest.

Abijoudi's was only one of Monrovia's many temptations. Going to a movie was next on our list. The James Bond thriller, "Dr. No," had finally made it to Liberia. Our friends were raving about the film. An effort had been made in the fifties to turn Fleming's novels into a TV series. The producers recruited an American actor for the Bond role and named him Jimmie. Can you imagine the line, "My name's Bond, Jimmy Bond." The series flopped.

We also discovered Oscar's, an excellent French restaurant that perched on the edge of the Atlantic in a beautiful setting. Oscar stood by our table and personally cooked flaming steak Diane with cognac. Later, a volunteer would catch amoebic dysentery at the restaurant and Oscar's was put on Peace Corps' ban list. Jo and I never ate the salad, never got dysentery and never obeyed the ban. Oscar's became a must-do on our Monrovia trips. After dinner we found a cozy bar tended by a big-busted German woman and Jo ordered a grasshopper, a frothy drink made with Crème de Menthe, Crème de Cacao and cream.

"A grasshopper," the woman shouted across the crowded room. "What's a hopper?" Everyone turned and stared at us as Jo Ann and I struggled to remember the ingredients. After that, Jo ordered more simple drinks.

Satiated and exhausted, we returned to the PC hostel. The next morning we caught a taxi back to Gbarnga and the quiet life.

CHAPTER 22

"WOE IS ME, SHAME AND SCANDAL IN THE FAMILY"

Morris dutifully showed up on our doorstep for his visit and Jo Ann cooked the duck she had bought at Abijoudi's. It was a multi-course production. She spent several hours hovering over our three-burner kerosene stove in an already hot and humid kitchen.

"Skinny duck," Morris had whined. I found Jo crying in the kitchen later. After that Morris got chop cooked by Sam when he visited. He was probably happier. Morris has little appreciation for gourmet. Three years later in a Washington DC hotel, Jo dumped a pitcher of ice water on his head.

"What was that for?" he yelled. "For the duck," had been the reply. It wasn't smart to mess with Jo. She was quick to remember and slow to forgive.

It was shortly after Morris's visit that I was knocked out by a diabolical tropical bug of unknown origin. It announced its presence with a low temperature of 100 degrees that soon climbed to 103. Normally it hovered around 101. Les Cohen, the Peace Corps doctor who lived in Gbarnga, came by and shrugged his shoulders a lot. He used the lottery approach to medicine. "Let's see if this works." We must have explored his whole medicine chest with minimal results.

As I mentioned earlier, there were no substitute teachers. Whenever a teacher was absent, the class was left to fend for itself. Often, my students would come by to check on how Teacha was doing. "How are you feeling Mr. Mekemson? When are you coming back to teach? Can't you teach us while you are sick?" There's nothing like thirty kids standing around your house and looking mournful to create guilt. But I resisted; I've never found martyrdom attractive.

For entertainment I tackled the locker of 100 books the Peace Corps provided to get Volunteers through slow days. Thomas Pynchon sucked me into his surreal world with his massive novel, "V." I'd read 50 pages and then take a nap.

A tribal woman provided distraction of another sort. Each morning around 10, she would stop in the dirt road opposite our house, squat down, and pee while looking at our screen door. I didn't have a clue to her motivation but I found myself looking forward to her visits. Maybe she was practicing Ju Ju (African magic medicine). Or maybe the location inspired her bladder. Who knows? I tried to pry out of Sam if she had an ulterior motive other than peeing, but he would just shake his head and mutter. Once he went charging out of our house and yelled at her in rapid fire Kpelle. She left but was back the next day.

Miranda Hall occupied my evenings. This popular bar and dance hall added significantly to my already splitting headache. Loudspeakers perched on top of the establishment blasted African High Life music for miles around. Since it was located one hundred yards from our house, we received the full benefit of its marketing campaign. One song I remember from hearing at least ten times a night had a country-western theme and a Jamaican origin: *Woe is me, shame and scandal in the family.*

Later, I actually witnessed a little shame and scandal in the house next to the bar. I was walking by when the 'man of the house' came down the street, nodded to me and went inside. It seems he was early. I heard a loud shout at the same time a well-endowed, totally erect, naked man burst through the screen window and hit the ground running. Right behind was the jilted husband. The two streaked by me and disappeared downtown. The naked guy was really fast.

Les was out of town when my illness decided to peak. As my temperature passed the 103 mark and headed for 104, I began to worry about hallucinating and becoming irrational. I asked Jo to send Sam over to fetch an Indian doctor who served the local community. Dr. Swami (yes that was his name) came right over.

"Here, drink this," he said.

Dr. Swami gave me a sweet, syrupy liquid that tasted great, knocked me out and cured me. The next morning I woke up feeling much better. I was even able to participate that weekend in a Thanksgiving feast that the upcountry Peace Corps' staff Bob Cohen and his wife hosted for the local Volunteers. The turkey tasted like sawdust due to the lingering remnants of my bug, but hey, who was complaining. There was a bottle of scotch to wash it down. I still have a photo where everyone is looking at the camera except Jo and me. We are looking at Johnny Walker. After the final sip, I was almost prepared to forgive Bob for not feeding us our first day in town.

The really big question that occupied my mind, now that I had recovered, was how my class had fared during my several weeks' absence. Would I return to a group of students eager to make up for lost time or an unruly mob prepared to sacrifice me to the jungle gods?

CHAPTER 23

READING AND WRITING AND ARITHMETIC TAUGHT TO THE TUNE OF AN EBONY STICK

The first 15 minutes at school answered the question. The class of moderately behaved students had morphed into a 30-headed monster. I was to be punished for being gone.

Considering the 15-year age difference between the youngest and oldest student, the kids were capable of several levels of mischief. After five days I had worked my way through every classroom management skill Peace Corps taught and several I made up. Nothing worked.

"They need to be whipped," my fellow Liberian teachers insisted. "That's what we do."

I patiently explained that Peace Corps teachers didn't whip their students. It was chiseled in stone. Eternal damnation and banishment to a very cold place would result.

"Then pretend you are going to whip them. Just don't do it," was the next helpful suggestion.

Being desperate and up for a little corruption, I thought about it. Where in the Peace Corps bible did it say that threats were out of line? After all, hadn't Teddy Roosevelt said, "Speak softly and carry a big stick?" So I went out in the jungle and cut one. Next I introduced it to my students.

"Oh, Mr. Mekemson, what a big stick you have," they said. I could see the respect shining in their eyes. I explained its purpose. They could behave and earn positive points or they could misbehave and earn negative points. If they earned enough negative points, the stick would be waiting. I didn't tell them it would take a combination of Al Capone and Count Dracula to reach the point total for punishment.

The system worked. Whenever the class bordered on chaos, I would head for the blackboard, chalk in hand. Instant silence resulted. It was 'Reading and writing and arithmetic taught to the tune of an ebony stick.' We started making up for lost time.

Of course there was an exception. Isn't there always? It came in the form of Mary, an 11-year old going on 13. Her uncle was principal of the high school and a Big Man in town so this meant *she* was important. No Liberian teacher would dare touch a stick to her ornery hide, so certainly a Peace Corps teacher wouldn't. She called my bluff and pushed her points right up to the rim. I urgently sought reasons to give her positive points, but the opportunities were few and far between. She went over the top and smugly whispered to her girlfriends to watch what would happen.

Now I had a real problem. Obviously I couldn't beat her. I am really not the beating kind. But neither could I ignore her. The end of the day came and I dismissed the class but asked her to stay. The students walked out the door and stopped on the other side. They weren't leaving. Nobody at the school was— including the teachers. They were all waiting to see what Mr. Mekemson would do.

Mr. Mekemson was worrying. That's what he was doing. I got out my big stick. Mary was no longer so nonchalant.

"Don't beat me Teacha, I beg you, don't beat me," she screamed and screamed and screamed. I gently touched her with my stick. You would have thought I was pulling all of her fingernails and half of her toenails out, slowly. I knew everyone in the school was listening in on this little drama and I imagined that half of Gbarnga was as well. *Oh boy*, I thought, *you have royally screwed up this time, Curtis.*

I mumbled something about the importance of changing her ways and sent her off. And then I waited. How long would it be before the Peace Corps jeep came by to carry Jo Ann and me away? The next day at school was quiet. Mary stayed home and I had a class of angels. Even other classes were quiet.

At noon, one of the Liberian teachers stopped by. She had a student she wanted me to beat. My response was not polite.

Two days later I received the message: John Bonal, Principal of Gboveh High School and Mary's uncle, wanted to see me. This was it. I prepared my case carefully. I didn't want to leave. A lovely war was waiting for me at home, and I had developed a considerable fondness for Liberia and its people. I went to see Mr. Bonal with all of the enthusiasm of a hippopotamus crossing the Sahara. He was smiling when I greeted him. I even managed to get a decent snap out of the handshake.

"I've heard about your reputation," he started and paused. Words like child beater, monster, and hater of kids roared through my mind. "And I would like you and your wife to come and teach at the high school. We think you would make a great addition to our faculty. We would like you to teach history and geography and Jo Ann to teach French and science."

Talk about surprise. Here I was prepared to be booted out of the country, ready to beg as the Liberians liked to say, ready to humble myself and crawl across the floor if need be, and I was being offered the opportunity to teach two of my favorite subjects.

"Sir, your niece..." I managed to stumble out.

Mr. Bonal's smile widened, "Ah yes," he said, "that was a good job. Now she will be a much better student."

Suddenly I had this suspicion that Mr. Bonal wanted me for a reason other than my 'great' teaching ability. I pictured myself practicing with a bull-whip out behind the high school as students lined up for their daily punishment. "Mr. Mekemson will see you now. Do you have any final words?"

But the offer was legitimate. After appearing to give it consideration for two seconds, I said yes. Jo Ann would have to speak for herself but I couldn't imagine her saying no. Actually, she took about five seconds to think through all of the ramifications. Her only complaint was that the history classes were assigned to me. She was the history major.

With my career as a high school teacher looming, I found it hard to concentrate on the second grade. I did manage to wrap up my final few weeks without whipping anyone else.

CHAPTER 24

I DO AWAY WITH SPOT

I did have a remaining *elementary* task. January was the Liberian School system's 'summer vacation.' Unfortunately, this didn't mean we were free to play like real teachers; Peace Corps expected first year Volunteers to take on a summer project.

Second year Volunteers, on the other hand, were allowed to treat their vacation as a vacation. Most of them flew off to East Africa and the big game parks.

Jo Ann decided to read to a blind student. Henrietta George lived on the Methodist compound. Reading a variety of books and magazines to her was a simple but worthwhile project that would brighten and broaden the young woman's world.

My decision was slightly more complicated. I decided to do away with Spot. Why shouldn't Liberian children have books that reflected their own culture as opposed to books that were based on Dick, Jane and their bouncy, four-legged companion? So I chose to write an elementary school Liberian reader. Peace Corps staff in Monrovia quickly approved the idea.

Immediately afterwards, I woke up at 3:00 a.m. wondering what the heck I had gotten myself into. My lack of knowledge about Liberian culture was only exceeded by my limited expertise in developmental reading skills. But second thoughts rarely stop me from plunging forward and this time was no exception. There were teaching guides to review, people to interview, folk tales to gather, and stories to write, rewrite and finish in simple English.

It turned into a massive project that occupied my full summer and beyond. Sam gathered several of his friends together to tell me African folktales they had learned around village cooking fires as young children. Most of the stories involved animals and included lessons on behavior.

Several were about the trickster Spider. Here's one I included in my reader.

How Spider Got His Small Waist

Spider was very greedy. He didn't share food and he didn't share money. He didn't share anything. He kept it all for himself. One day a group of villagers came to visit Spider.

"We are having a feast. Would you like to come?" they asked.

"Oh yes," Spider answered with joy as he rubbed his eight legs together. "I will be glad to eat your food."

Shortly after, people from another village knocked on his door. They, too, were having a feast on the same day, and Spider was invited. Of course he would come. He never missed a free meal. But how could he make sure he stuffed himself with food at both feasts? He thought and he thought.

Suddenly he jumped up and did a dance. "I know what I can do!" he sang.

Spider found two very long ropes. He tied one to his door and then walked to the first village and gave the people the other end. "When the feast is ready, tug on the rope," he told them. Spider then did the same thing with the second village.

When Spider got back to his hut he tied both ropes around his waist. "Now I am ready," he thought. "When the first feast starts I will run to the village and eat as much of their food as I can gulp down." (Spider could gulp very fast.) "When the second village tugs on my rope, I will run there and eat all of the bananas."

Spider was quite pleased with his plan, but all of his work had made him very tired. He fell into his bed and snored loudly. He was dreaming about a large dish of palm butter and rice when a tug on his waist woke him up. "Dinner!" he shouted.

He was just outside of his hut when the second village tugged on its rope. Oh no! Both feasts were happening at once. But that wasn't the really bad part. With both villages tugging on him, Spider could not move. He was going to miss both feasts.

"Where's Spider?" the villagers at the first feast worried. Everyone in the village grabbed the rope and tugged as hard as they could.

"Spider is going in the wrong direction!" the people in the second village yelled. Everyone grabbed the rope and began pulling. Even the children helped. It was a tug of war between the two villages and Spider was caught in the middle! The ropes pulled tighter and tighter around him, squeezing his big belly in half.

And that, my friends, is how Spider got his small waist.

I liked the story. Students could relate and have fun with it. If the teacher had a rope, she could even divide her class and play tug of war.

In addition to folktales, I wrote several stories about the everyday life of the children. One series had them finding a large snake, another playing football (soccer). I even sent them off to Monrovia to visit a favorite uncle.

Finally, I wrapped up the book. I did a final rewrite of the stories and shipped them off to Peace Corps headquarters in Monrovia. And then I waited. I was nervous. I felt like a new author who had sent his work off to a publisher or an agent for the first time. I had devoted hundreds of hours to a project that might come to nothing.

Two weeks later I heard back from Monrovia. Peace Corps staff liked the book, apparently a lot. A Peace Corps Volunteer with editing experience would be partnered with a curriculum expert to prepare the book for publishing. A Volunteer who was an artist would add illustrations. The book was to become a Department of Education project. None of our names would be included. I was fine with that. Or let me put it another way. My ego wasn't too bruised. The satisfaction was in knowing that the book would be used in classrooms. Dick, Jane and Spot could retire to California.

Then WAWA (a term coined by experienced African hands that stood for West Africa Wins Again) struck. The book wouldn't be published at all. I had made the mistake of assuming the government would support a reader that featured Liberian children instead of Dick, Jane and Spot. I understood I might be criticized for inaccurately portraying Liberians or missing the target on developmental reading skills. But these were things that could be fixed.

What I had failed to understand was just how paranoid the Americo-Liberians were about maintaining power. The reader was apparently a dangerous revolutionary tract that would help tribal Liberian children develop a sense of identity and pride. They might grow up and challenge the government. Peace Corps staff told me to drop the project and to pretend it had never happened. To do otherwise was my one-way ticket home.

I was angry. I went back and reread what I had written. Yes, it featured tribal children and tribal folktales but there was nothing revolutionary about the book. Not one word criticized President Tubman, the True Whig Party or the Liberian government.

On the other hand the book didn't praise President Tubman, the True Whig Party or the Liberian Government. To be published, the reader evidently needed to be a propaganda piece, and that I was unwilling to write.

CHAPTER 25

HOW BRUNHILDA THE CAT BECAME RASPUTIN

A new house came with the new teaching position. It was located on the United States Agency for International Development (USAID) compound, two hundred yards away from the high school and about the same distance from where the Peace Corps' staff lived. Mr. Bonal was our neighbor.

Our new home was quite luxurious; it had electricity, running water and a real toilet— located out the back door in its own little house. The days of cockroaches playing tag on our butts were past. I flushed the toilet over and over again just to watch the water go down. It even had a cement bathtub that featured cold water and toads.

The one thing the house needed desperately was a paint job; the previous occupants had felt that purple, green and yellow were quite attractive. Painting the house was added to our growing list of summer projects. So was childcare. One of the second year Peace Corps couples, Dick and Sandy Robb, left their four little female kittens to live with us while they flew off to East Africa. We became substitute parents. Our pay was to have the pick of the litter. Great.

I built our temporarily adopted cat family a three-story mansion out of cardboard. It was a maze of rooms, hanging toys, hallways and ramps. The kittens would disappear inside and play for long periods. We could hear them banging around as they stalked each other and attacked the hanging toys.

In a creative moment inspired by the evening cocktail hour, we decided to use the house as an intelligence test to determine which kitten we would keep. First we waited until the kittens were appropriately hungry, and then we brewed up their favorite meal, fish head stew. Here's the recipe. Take several ripe fish heads and throw them in a pan of boiling water. When their eyes pop out, they're done.

Next, we encouraged the kittens to sniff their gourmet dinner and showed them that the meal would be located just outside the ground floor door of their mansion. Now we were ready for the test. Each kitten would be placed inside the third story door and given a nudge. We would then close the door and time how long it took the kitten to reach the banquet. Our theory was that the kitten with the quickest time through the maze of hallways and ramps would be the brightest.

Grey Kitten # 1 was a pudgy little character that never missed a meal. My money was riding on her. She breezed through the maze in three minutes sharp and set the time to beat. There was a chance that the sound of her munching away on fish heads might inspire the other kittens on to even greater glory, however.

Grey Kitten #2 was one of those 'whatever it is you want me to do I am going to do the opposite' type cats. Not surprisingly, she strolled out of the door seven minutes later and ignored the food altogether. (Afterwards, we were to speculate that she was the most intelligent cat and blew the race because she had no intention of living with someone who made her go through a maze for dinner.)

Grey Kitten #3 was the lean and mean version. Scrawny might be a better description. She obviously needed dinner the most and proved her mettle by blazing through the house in two minutes. The contest was all but over.

Kitten # 4 was what pollsters normally classify as 'other.' To start with, she was yellow instead of grey. She was also loud. In honor of her operatic qualities, Jo had named her Brunhilda. By the time her turn came up, she was impatiently scratching the hand that was about to feed her and growling in a demonic way. I gladly shoved the little monster through the third story door and closed it. We heard a scrabbling on the other side as tiny claws dug into the cardboard floor. Her race down the first hall was punctuated by a crash on the other end. Brake problems.

Then she was up and running again, but it sounded like toward us. Had her crash disoriented her? Suddenly the third story door burst open and one highly focused yellow kitty went flying through the air. She made a perfect four point landing and dashed to the dinner dish. Her time? Ten seconds.

And that is how Brunhilda came to be our cat. Our decision to keep her led us to turn her over and check out her brunhildahood a little more closely. Turns out she had a couple of furry little protuberances where there shouldn't have been any. Like Dr. Gibbs' cat, she was a he. In honor of Brunhilda's demonic growl and generally obnoxious behavior, we renamed the kitten Rasputin after the nefarious Russian monk.

CHAPTER 26

DO YOUR PART—THE GOOD DOG

The conclusion of our other vacation project, the painting of our green, purple and orange house, was much more satisfying than my second grade reader. I started by buying a case of Club Beer. I didn't know much about painting, but I knew house painters found inspiration in hops.

While I was sipping a brew and pondering what paint best covered purple, Mr. Bonal came over and assured me there wasn't anything that a bucket of white wash couldn't cure. Jo and I dutifully trotted down to the Lebanese store and were soon applying white wash with our broom. We were quite pleased with the finished project and ourselves.

As our summer vacation drew to a close, we started preparing for our career as high school teachers, where I would continue my efforts to get booted out of the country. But that's a story for later in the book. First I am going to share tales about our everyday life in Liberia. I'll talk about the animals that amused us, look into tribal culture, discuss the creepy, crawly things that exist in a tropical jungle and tell about our escape to East Africa for a 2500 mile safari in a VW Beetle.

As for the animals, you are about to meet Do Your Part the good dog, Boy the bad dog, Rasputin the terrorist cat, and Rooster, the foulest of fowls. Consider this the Alf Wight, aka James Herriot, section of my book.

John Bonal lived in a cement-block house that was the twin of ours. His brother's family lived behind the house in an attached shed. Being successful in Liberia meant that your relatives came over and lived with you. It was the ultimate share-the-wealth-social-welfare program. Part of John's extended family included three dogs creatively named Puppy Doodle, Brownie Girl and Do Your Part. They came over to watch the white washing action and decided to stay. They became our extended family. We fed them. If I have my genealogy correct, Brownie Girl was Do Your Part's mom who in turn was Puppy Doodle's mother.

This three-generation family dug foxholes around the outside of our house and quickly established that they were our pets. Other dogs need not apply. Mr. Bonal's brother was more than happy to have us take over feeding responsibilities and Rasputin was pleased to have someone to terrorize. So everyone was happy.

Do Your Part took things a step further and became 'my' dog. She was a charming little Basenji with impeccable manners. Everywhere I went, she went, including school. Normally, this amused my students. I would walk into the class with DYP a respectful three feet behind. She would immediately arrange herself under my desk and quietly remain there until I left the classroom.

This worked fine until she had puppies. They started following her as soon as they could walk the 100 yards to the school. Then I would arrive in my class followed by DYP who in turn was followed by four puppies. It was quite the parade. Unfortunately, the puppies lacked Do Your Part's decorum and considered the classroom a playpen. The students decided it was not an appropriate learning environment and I had to agree. DYP and company had to go. It was not a happy parting.

"Take your puppies and go," I ordered firmly. Do Your Part looked at me in disbelief.

"Out!" I said.

Sad eyes stared back accusingly. But I held firm. She didn't let it get her down, however. As soon as the puppies had departed, she was back in class. One time her insistence on following me had more drastic consequences.

Gbarnga had a sizeable population of Mandingoes, most of whom were Muslims. They had been gradually sifting into Liberia from across the Guinea border. Originally the Americo-Liberians had blocked their entrance to the country, fearing they might pose a threat to their power. American Missionary influence may also have played a role. President Tubman changed the policy. By the time we had arrived, the number of Mandingos had reached the point where they decided to build a mosque in town. I'd wander over on occasion to check their progress. The mosque was an impressive building by Gbarnga standards, easily five times larger than any other structure on the main road.

At last the day came for its grand opening. Having watched the mosque being built, I decided it would be interesting to attend the festivities. I put on my tie, grabbed our two cameras and headed out the door. Do Your Part was waiting and ready to go along.

This was not a Do Your Part type of celebration, however. Muslims aren't particularly fond of dogs and consider them unclean. I figured this meant they didn't want any dogs, even polite dogs, attending their holy ceremony. I suggested to Do Your Part she stay home. Fat chance. I walked 100 yards and glanced back over my shoulder. There was DYP, slinking along behind. I knew there was no way I would make it to the ceremony without a little brown dog lurking in the background.

Do Your Part would have to be left in our house. The action was drastic; the only time we let her in was to eat dead insects in the evening. She would come in just before we went to bed and wander around crunching down sausage bugs. It eliminated sweeping. She had never been locked inside.

Since Jo was reading to her blind friend, and Sam was off for the day, I couldn't even leave her with company. I reluctantly shoved her in the house and walked off to the sounds of doggy protest. It seemed to work. I reached the mosque just as the outside ceremonies were concluding and people were preparing to move inside. Dignitaries were everywhere. It was my intention to hang out on the periphery and remain inconspicuous. This is hard when you are the only white person in the crowd and you have two cameras hanging around your neck.

It took about thirty seconds for a tall, official looking man in a white robe to approach me and express in broken English how pleased he was that the international press from Monrovia had decided to cover the event. While I struggled to inform him that I was only a local Peace Corps Volunteer, he ushered me into the mosque to a seat of honor. I looked around nervously. The podium was about 10 feet away and I was in the front row.

A hush descended on the crowd as an obviously important dignitary approached the podium. Liberia's top Muslim Cleric had come to town to officiate at the opening ceremony. He gave me his best media smile and I dutifully took his picture.

Unexpectedly, there was a disturbance at the back of the mosque. Several men were trying to capture a little brown dog that was deftly eluding them and was making a beeline for me. Do Your Part had managed to escape from the house. Now she was escaping from half of Islam. In seconds that seemed like hours she was in front of me, wagging her tail and prancing around like she hadn't seen me in six months. Hot on her tail were three huge Mandingo men.

"Is this your dog?" their leader managed to stammer out in barely repressed fury as he gave DYP a tentative boot on the butt. Happily, she figured out that the situation was hazardous and decided there were other parts of town she wanted to see. I was amazed at her ability to avoid lunging people. I dearly wished I could have escaped with her. It wasn't to be. It was my job to stay behind and be glared at. I was so embarrassed, I didn't remember a single part of the ceremony.

Later, when I arrived home, Do Your Part was outside the house, all wiggles and waggles, obviously no worse for her adventure. Jo Ann greeted me.

"It was the strangest thing when I got home," she said. "Do Your Part was inside and frantic to get out. When I let her loose she took off like our house was on fire. I wonder if Sam let her in by mistake." The best laid plans of mice and men…

CHAPTER 27

BOY—THE BAD DOG

Boy was a large, brindle dog with questionable parentage and a serious problem. He didn't like black people. He lived with a Peace Corps Volunteer named Holly, who also had a dog named Lolita. Boy came into our life when Lolita had puppies and drove him off. She believed he would eat her children.

Boy went out looking for other white people to live with and found Jo Ann and me.

Normally, I wouldn't have cared. One more dog wasn't going to make much difference given our menagerie of three dogs and Rasputin the Cat. It was Boy's attitude that bothered me. It wasn't very Peace Corps-like to have your dog attack Liberians when they came to visit.

Boy also had an issue with Rasputin; he regarded him as prey. I initiated several civil discussions with the dog about his bad habits and suggested he might end up in Liberian soup, but all he did was growl. Once, when he had Rasputin cornered, I slapped him on the butt. He almost took my hand off. Consequently, I wasn't sympathetic when the soldiers arrived.

They were standing outside our house, waving their guns around, when Jo and I came home from teaching.

"What's up?" I asked in my most official Peace Corps voice. You learned early on not to mess with Liberian soldiers. There was a reason why the government refused to issue them bullets.

"Your dog ate one of the Superintendent's guinea fowl," their sergeant mumbled ominously. The Superintendent of Bong County was the equivalent to a governor except that he had more power. He lived a quarter mile away and his guinea fowl strutted around freely in the government compound.

"Which one?" I asked innocently.

"What does it matter which guinea fowl the dog ate?" Sarge sneered.

"No, no," I responded, "I meant which dog?"

He glared at me for a moment and then pointed at Boy. I relaxed. It didn't seem like Do Your Part, Brownie Girl or Puppy Doodle would have done in the Superintendent's guinea fowl. They were three of the best-fed dogs in Gbarnga.

"Why don't you arrest him?" I offered hopefully.

"Not him," he shouted. "You. You come with us!" Seemingly, the interview wasn't going the way the soldier wanted. A Liberian might have been beaten by then. I decided it was time to end the conversation.

"Look," I said, "that dog does not belong to me. He belongs across town. I am not going anywhere with you." With that I walked into our house and closed the door. It was risky but not as risky as going off with the soldiers. They grumbled around outside for a while and finally left.

Jo and I relaxed "small," as the Liberians would say, but really didn't feel safe until that evening. It was a six-beer night. Finally, around 10:00 p.m., we went to bed believing we had beaten the rap.

WHAM! WHAM! WHAM!

"What in the hell was that?" I yelled as I jumped out of bed. It was pitch black and 4:00 a.m. in the morning.

WHAM! WHAM! WHAM!

"Someone is pounding on our back door," Jo Ann whispered, sounding as frightened as I felt.

I grabbed our baseball bat, headed for the door, and yanked it open. Soldiers were everywhere. The same friendly sergeant from the night before was standing there with the butt of his rifle poised to strike our door again.

"Your dog ate another one of the Superintendent's guinea fowls," he proclaimed to the world. I could tell he was ecstatic about the situation. He had probably tossed the bird over the fence to Boy.

"This time you *are* going with us," he growled.

In addition to being frightened, I was growing tired of the routine. "I am sorry you are having such a hard time guarding guinea fowls," I said, trying to sound reasonable, "but I explained to you yesterday that the dog does not belong to me and I am not going anywhere with you. Ask Mr. Bonal and he will tell you the dog is not ours."

Sometimes the ballsy approach is your best option. Sometimes it isn't.

I closed the door and held my breath. Sarge was not happy. He and his soldiers buzzed around outside like angry hornets. Still, yanking a Peace Corps Volunteer out of his house and dragging him off in the middle of the night over a guinea fowl could have serious consequences, much more serious than merely reporting back that I was uncooperative. I could see the headlines:

Soldiers Beats Peace Corps Volunteer Because Dog Eats Guinea Fowl. Liberian Ambassador Called to White House to Explain.

That would have been right up there with "Peace Corps Volunteer Beaten because Dog Invades Mosque!" How did I get myself into these things? I hoped the sergeant shared my perspective. At a minimum, I figured he would check with Bonal. John might not appreciate being awakened in the middle of the night, but it would serve him right for laughing when I had told him the guinea fowl story the night before. Anyway, I suspected he was up and watching the action.

We had a very nervous thirty minutes before the soldiers finally marched off. In the US, this is the point where you would be calling your attorney, your mother, and the local TV station. Here, my only backups were the Peace Corps representative and doctor: one to represent me, the other to patch me back together.

Happily, our part of the ordeal was over. It turned out that Peter, a young Liberian who worked for Holly, actually owned Boy. The soldiers finally had someone they could bully.

Peter was pulled into court and fined for Boy's heinous crimes. Boy, in turn, was sold to some villagers to cover the cost of the fine. As for Boy's fate, he was guest of honor at a village feast. Being a bad dog in Liberia had rather serious consequences.

CHAPTER 28

RASPUTIN AND THE COCKLE DOODLE ROOSTER

I never imagined that a rooster and a cat might collaborate, but when the rooster next door took over Rasputin's job of waking us up at 5:30 every morning, it almost changed my mind.

Rasputin had grown into one fine tomcat, *sweet meat* as my students said. He did not grieve over Boy's untimely demise. Now Rasputin could resume his role as Dominant Animal. His primary responsibility under this job title was *Dog Stalker*. You knew when he was working. The neighborhood dogs carefully avoided the tall clumps of grass where he liked to hide. Rasputin was particularly obnoxious when the wind was whipping up a storm. He would hide downwind and make it difficult for the dogs to sniff him out. I felt sorry for the poor dog that came too close.

A streak of yellow tomcat and a yip of doggy surprise proclaimed Rasputin's attack. What made his behavior particularly strange was that he came at the dogs on his two hind legs, walking upright. This allowed both front legs to be used as slashing weapons. It was a wise dog that steered clear of the Kung Fu Cat.

This wasn't Rasputin's only trick. He could also do flips. I had taught him how and was quite proud of my accomplishment. Each night Rasputin and I would head for the bedroom where I would flip him several times in a row on the bed. He was usually good for about ten before he would attack me, thus signaling that the game was over. Jo thought it was cruel but I told her it was quality bonding-time. It also turned out to be a valuable skill.

One evening when the ricebirds were returning to their nests, we saw a yellow flash out the window. Rasputin leapt into the air, did a flip and came down with bird a la carte. After that, I figured Rasputin had graduated so we didn't practice anymore.

Another game we played was 'leap-snake.' It was quite similar to leapfrog except the objective was to teach Rasputin how to avoid snakes and to see how high he could jump in the air. On a good night he would clear five feet.

The rules of the game were simple. I would detach the spring from our screen door and roll it across the floor. Rasputin, who had a Liberian's instincts, assumed that anything long and twisty was a snake and that all snakes were deadly poisonous. His response was to shoot straight into the air and land several feet away. It was one of those situations where you leap first and ask questions later. In this case, Rasputin was guilty of jumping to the wrong conclusions.

Rasputin spent his nights outside fulfilling tomcat duties, but by 5:30 in the morning he was demanding we let him in. He did this by practicing his operatic meows under our bedroom window. Since no amount of suggesting that he should learn from Boy's experience discouraged him, I jumped out of bed one morning and chased him across the yard. This got Jo Ann excited– our cat was going to run away and never come back! Jo may also have been concerned about the neighbor's reaction to my charging out of the house naked. That type of thing bothered her. I promised to repent and assured her that the cat would be back in time for dinner. He was.

It is at this point that Rasputin's working relationship with the Cockle Doodle Rooster developed. It's my theory that Rasputin subcontracted with the noisy fowl to wake us up when his tomcatting responsibilities kept him out late. I didn't make this correlation until the rooster crowed directly under our window one morning at 5:30. Even then, I thought it was just a coincidence until the rooster repeated himself the next morning. It wasn't just the crowing that irritated me; it was the nature of the crow. American and European roosters go *cock-a-doodle-do*. Even urban children know this because that's how it is spelled out in books. Liberian roosters go *cock-a-doodle*— and stop. You are constantly waiting for the other '*do*' to drop.

"This crowing under our window," I thought to myself, "has to be nipped in the bud."

That evening I filled a bucket with water and put it next to my bed. Sure enough, at 5:30 the next morning there he was: "COCK-A-DOODLE!" I jumped up, grabbed my bucket, and threw the water out the window on the unsuspecting fowl. "Squawk!" I heard, as one very wet and irritated rooster headed home as fast as his little rooster legs could carry him.

"Chicken!" I yelled out after his departing body. "And that," I said to Jo Ann, "should be the end of that particular problem."

I was inspired though. Cats don't think much of getting wet either. What if I kept a bucket of water next to the bed and dumped it on Rasputin the next time he woke us up. Jo couldn't even blame me for running outside naked. With warm thoughts of having solved two problems with one bucket, I went to bed that night loaded for cat, so to speak.

"COCK-A-DOODLE!" roared the rooster outside our window precisely at 5:30 a.m.

"Damn," I thought, "that boy is one slow learner."

I fell out of bed, grabbed the bucket and dashed for the window. *There was no rooster there.* I looked up and spotted him about half the way to Bonal's house. He was running at full tilt across the yard away from our window. He had sneaked up on us, crowed and taken off! My opinion of the rooster took a paradigm leap. Here was one worthy opponent. The question was how to respond.

It took me a couple of days of devious thinking to arrive at a solution. What would happen if I recorded the rooster on a tape recorder and then played it back to him? I had a hand-held recorder that I used for exchanging letters with my dad, so I set myself the task of capturing the rooster's fowl language one afternoon. Since he had an extensive harem he liked to crow about, it wasn't long before I had a dozen or so *cock-a-doodles* on tape. I rewound the recorder, set it down inside our front screen door, cranked up the volume, and hit play.

The results were hilarious. Within seconds the rooster was on our porch, jumping up and down and screaming '*cock-a-doodle*.' There was a rooster inside of our house that had invaded *his* territory and he was going to tear him apart, *feather-by-feather*. Laughing, I picked up the recorder, rewound it, carried to the back screen door, and hit the play button again.

"*Cock-a-doodle, cock-a-doodle, cock-a-doodle*," I could hear the rooster as he roared around to the back of house to get at his implacable foe. Back and forth I went, front to back, back to front. And around and around the house the rooster went, flinging out his challenges. Finally, having laughed myself to exhaustion, I took pity on my feathered friend and shut the recorder off. This just about concludes the rooster story, but not quite.

One Friday evening, Jo and I had been celebrating the end of another week with gin and tonics until the wee hours, when we decided to see how the rooster would respond to his nemesis at one o'clock in the morning. Considering our 5:30 a.m. wakeup calls, we felt there was a certain amount of justice in the experiment. I set up the recorder and played a "*Cock-a-doodle*."

"COCK-A-DOODLE!" was the immediate response. No challenge was to go unanswered. "*Cock-a-doodle*" we heard as roosters from the Superintendent's compound checked in. "*Cock-a-doodle, cock-a-doodle*" we heard in the distance as town roosters rose to the challenge. Soon every rooster in Gbarnga was awake, and probably every resident.

Jo and I decided to keep our early morning rooster-arousing episode to ourselves.

CHAPTER 29

CULTURE SHOCK AND 'GOING BUSH'

Joining the Peace Corps should come with a label like they put on cigarette packs. It would read *"Warning: This experience may change your concept of reality."*

Our vision of the world is shaped through culturally tinted glasses. Not surprisingly, the reality of our parents and our society becomes our reality. It's very hard to imagine life from any other perspective. Close encounters with other cultures can shake this vision, but not easily. We wear our culture like bulletproof vests, rarely allowing a stray thought to penetrate. Or we focus so hard on extolling our own culture that we fail to learn valuable lessons another culture may teach us.

A key element of our Peace Corps training had been to instill cultural sensitivity. Eugene Burdick and William Lederer's book, *The Ugly American,* was published in 1958. It made a significant impression on me. US citizens were known for being pushy and acting superior in dealing with foreign cultures. Both behaviors created enemies. The Peace Corps' job was to make friends and provide aid, not alienate people.

There was another important reason for the Peace Corps cross-cultural training. Risks are involved when you run headlong into another culture. Depression is one. The environment may be so totally different that it becomes disorienting. The common name for this is culture shock. Learning about Liberia and its tribes was a form of inoculation.

My transition from California to Liberia was relatively smooth. At first, Gbarnga didn't seem all that different from my old hometown of Diamond Springs. A small rural town is a small rural town. I suffered more shock going from Sierra College to UC Berkeley than I did going from Berkeley to Liberia. My disorientation (and depression) would wait until I returned to the US.

A less common phenomenon is going native, or 'bush' as it was called in Liberia. In this instance, you become so enthralled with the new culture that you adopt it as your own. There was a joke that circulated among Peace Corps Volunteers on how to determine when you were teetering on the edge.

Stage One: You arrive 'in country' and a fly lands in your coffee. You throw the coffee away, wash your cup, and pour yourself a new cup.

Stage Two: You've been there a few months and a fly lands in your coffee. You carefully pick the fly out with your spoon and then drink the coffee.

Stage Three: It's been over a year and you have become a grizzled veteran. A fly lands in your coffee. You yank it out with your fingers, squeeze any coffee it may have consumed back into the cup, toss the fly and then drink the coffee.

Stage Four: You've been there too long. A fly lands in your coffee cup. You yank the fly out, pop it into your mouth and throw the coffee away. It's time to go home. (In fact, I never met a Liberian who ate flies but bug-a-bugs, aka termites, were considered a real delicacy.)

If Peace Corps Volunteers had a tough time with culture shock and going bush, the tribal Liberians had a tougher one. Traditional cultures have never fared well in their confrontation with Western cultures. It isn't that our culture is so great; it's just that our technology is so glitzy. How do you keep young people 'down on the farm' when they hear the taxi horn blowing? And there were lots of taxis and money-busses in Gbarnga offering one-way trips to Monrovia.

Gbarnga was on the frontier of cultural change. On the surface, life could appear quite westernized. An occasional John Wayne movie even made it to town. My students would walk stiff-legged down Gbarnga's main street and do a great imitation of the Duke. They daydreamed about traveling to America where they would swagger down dusty streets and knock off bad guys with their trusty six shooters. (Or, more likely, where they would live in nice homes, drive fancy cars, and make lots of money.)

In town, loud speakers blared out music at decibel levels the Grateful Dead would have killed for while Lebanese shops pushed everything from Argentinean canned beef to London Dry Gin. The epitome of Americana, a Coca Cola sign, dominated the road as you left town on your way to Ganta.

William Tubman had been the first Americo-Liberian President to actively encourage tribal Liberians to shed their traditional cultures and become more Westernized, or at least more Liberian. His first push had been to encourage an increase in the number of missionaries working upcountry. They were welcome to proselytize whatever brand of Christianity they wished as long as they remembered, "to render unto Caesar that which was Caesar's."

We had enough US-based churches in Gbarnga to satisfy Pat Robertson. Missionaries were everywhere. Baptists and Catholics and Episcopalians and Presbyterians and other Christian groups worked the streets in unending competition to recruit African souls.

I was out on a bush walk several miles from town once when I spotted a man coming toward me dressed up in a coat and tie, wearing shiny black shoes, and carrying a brief case. My first reaction was to get off the trail. I was too slow.

"Wait, I have something to give you," he called.

You can bet that reassured me. But I waited. Standing there in the middle of a muddy trail in the middle of the African jungle, the man very carefully opened his brief case and pulled out a magazine. The headline screamed,

"The World Is Coming to an End" and apparently I was too. The magazine was *Awake*; a Jehovah Witness had me in his clutches.

Sometimes, if I closed my eyes and pretended, I could almost believe I was home. Almost. Then Africa would whip around and bite me. Sure, the local villagers would dutifully file in to church on Sunday morning and pray for blessings the way their western counterparts did. But Sunday afternoon might find them out sacrificing a chicken to make sure God got the message. And yes, there was a Coca Cola sign on the way to Ganta, but next to it was a tall tree where you could find offerings to the spirit that lived in the tree.

The Bush Devil would further convince me about the difference between African reality and my own.

CHAPTER 30

BUSH DEVILS, JUJU, AND LIGHTNING MEN

Sam spent hours listening to the Kingston Trio on our record player and took to peanut butter and jelly sandwiches like a cat takes to birds. Western culture fired his imagination and tantalized his taste buds, but Kpelle culture was an integral part of who he was. He even had the scars to prove it. They marched down his chest in two neat rows.

"How did you get those," Jo asked with ten percent concern and ninety percent curiosity.

"I can't tell you," Sam replied with obvious nervousness as Jo's eyebrows rose. "But I can tell Mr. Mekemson."

Aha, I thought, Sam and I belong to the same organization, the Men's Club! Actually Sam belonged to a very exclusive men's organization, the Poro Society, which I wasn't allowed to belong to. Its functions were to pass on tribal traditions, teach useful skills, and keep errant tribe members in line. Everything about the organization was hush-hush. Tribal members who revealed secrets could be banned and even executed.

Political power on the local level was closely tied to membership in the Poro Society. On the national level, President Tubman assumed leadership of all Poro Societies in Liberia. Tribal women had a similar secret organization called the Sande Society, which prepared young women for adulthood and marriage. A controversial aspect of the Sande initiation ceremony was female genital mutilation– cutting off the clitoris.

Sam got off easy.

He had been to Bush School the previous summer and learned how to be a good Kpelle man. Graduation to adulthood consisted of an all-consuming encounter with the Poro Society's Bush Devil. It ate him. Sam went to Bush School as a child and was spit out as a man. The scarification marks had been left by the devil's 'teeth.' It seemed like a tough way to achieve adulthood, but at least it was fast and definitive. Maybe we should introduce the process to our kids in the US and skip the teenage years. Think of all of the angst it would avoid.

The Bush Devil was a very important tribal figure who was part religious leader, part cultural cop and part political hack. Non-Kpelle types and women weren't allowed to see him. When the Devil came to visit outlying villages, a frontman preceded him and ran circles around the local PCV's house while blowing a whistle. The Volunteer was expected to go inside, shut the door, close the shutters and stay there. No peeking.

We did get to see a Grebo Devil once. The Grebo Tribe was less secretive, or at least more mercenary. Some Peace Corps Volunteers had hired the local Devil for a Haight-Ashbury style African party. It was, after all, 1967, the "summer of love" in San Francisco and the "Dawning of the Age of Aquarius." Along with several other Volunteers, we hired a money bus to get to the party. Had we been thinking, we would have painted the bus with Day-Glo.

The Devil was all decked out in his regalia. His persona was somewhere between a voodoo nightmare and walking haystack. Grebo men scurried in front of him with brooms, clearing his path and grunting a lot. We stayed out of the way and took pictures.

Another area where Sam showed his tribal side was his fear of the newly dead. As I mentioned earlier, a person's spirit was considered particularly powerful and dangerous right after he or she died. Later, the spirit would move away into the bush and fade. But first it had to be tamed with appropriate mourning, an all-night bash. One didn't take chances. When Sam worked late for us after someone had died, he would borrow a knife and a flashlight in case he had to fight off the malevolent ghost on his way home. I had grown up next to a graveyard and was sympathetic with his concern.

Juju, or African witch doctor medicine, was another area where African reality varied from modern Western reality. Late one evening, in the middle of a tropical downpour, one of my high school students appeared on our doorstep very wet and very frightened. Mamadee Wattee was running for student body president. His opponent had purchased 'medicine' from a Juju man to make him sick.

It was serious business; people were known to die in similar circumstances. Had the opposition slandered Mamadee or stuffed the ballot box, I could have helped, but countering a magic potion wasn't taught at Berkeley, at least not officially. I took the issue to Mr. Bonal and he dealt with it. Mamadee stayed well and won the election.

The use of Juju medicine represents the darker side of tribal culture. Human body parts derived from ritual human sacrifice are reputed to be particularly effective in creating potions. Cannibalism may be involved. On the lighter side, my students once obtained a less potent 'medicine' and buried it under the goal post on the football (soccer) field with the belief that it would cause the other team to miss goals. It wasn't potent enough; the other team won.

Mamadee was also the reason behind our introduction to the Lightning Man. When Jo and I went on vacation to East Africa, we left Mamadee with $50 to buy a 50-gallon drum of kerosene. When we returned there was neither kerosene nor $50, but Mamadee was waiting. Someone had stolen the money and Mamadee was extremely upset. Fifty dollars represented a month's income for a Kpelle farmer. Mamadee's father, a chief of the Kpelle tribe, was even more upset and wanted to assure us that his son had nothing to do with the missing fortune. It was a matter of honor. He offered to have Mamadee submit to the Lightning Man to prove his innocence.

The Lightning Man had a unique power; he could make lighting strike whoever was guilty of a crime. If someone stole your cow or your spouse, zap! Since we were in the tropics, there was lots of lightning. Whenever anyone was struck, people would shake their heads knowingly. Another bad guy had been cooked; justice had been served.

We didn't believe Mamadee had taken the money, and even if he had, we certainly didn't want him fried, or even singed. We passed on the offer. The Chief insisted on giving us $50 to replace the stolen money.

Another Liberian Peace Corps Volunteer in a similar situation chose a different path. Here's how the story was told to us. The Volunteer had just purchased a brand new $70 radio so he could listen to the BBC and keep track of what was happening in the world. The money represented close to half of the Volunteer's monthly income. He had owned his bright, shiny, new toy for two days when it disappeared.

"I am going to get my radio back," he announced to anyone who would listen and then walked into the village where he quickly gathered some of his students to take him to the Lightning Man. Off he and half the town went, winding through the rainforest to the Lighting Man's hut. The Volunteer took out five dollars and gave it to the Lighting Man. (Lighting Men have to eat too.)

"I want you to make lighting strike whoever stole my radio," he said.

The Volunteer and his substantial entourage then returned home. By this time, everyone in the village knew about the trip, including, undoubtedly, the person who had stolen the radio.

That night, there was a tremendous thunder and lightning storm. Ignoring for the moment that it was in the middle of the rainy season and there were always tremendous thunder and lightning storms, place yourself in the shoes of the thief who believed in the Lightning Man's power. Each clap of thunder would have been shouting his name.

In the morning the Volunteer got up, had breakfast and went out on his porch. There was his radio. If all of this seems bizarre, the case of the woman who wore no underpants is even stranger.

CHAPTER 31

TRIAL BY POISONOUS LEAVES AND A RED HOT MACHETE

While the Lighting Man provided a hit-or-miss opportunity for taking out bad guys, a more formal means of determining guilt and innocence was achieved by asking the tribal judge, the Sassywood Man, to resolve the issue. This tribal official obtained his name through use of poisonous leaves from the Sassywood tree. The accused person was invited to chew a few. If he died, he was guilty. No DAs, lawyers or juries were needed.

Modern society frowns upon trial by survival, however. The Sassywood Man had been forced to come up with a new way of determining guilt. As it turned out, the father of one of my students, Amani Page, was the local tribal judge and Jo and I were privileged to witness an actual trial.

It all started with Amani showing up at our house at one in the afternoon on a Saturday in the middle of the dry season. His father was about to start a trial. Would we like to see it? There was no hesitation on our part even though it meant like 'mad dogs and Englishmen' we had to forgo our afternoon siesta and go out in the tropical sun.

As we headed west across town through the stifling heat, Amani provided background on the case. The plaintiff's wife had come home in the evening after a hard day of selling oranges at the market and told her husband that three men had accused her of not wearing underpants. This was serious slander suggestive of loose behavior, and the husband had filed charges through Liberia's western-type court system.

But there was a potential problem: what if the men knew something about his wife's behavior he didn't? Perhaps she was lying to him. If he lost the suit, he would have to pay all of the court costs, and be subject to counter-suits. He decided to hedge his bet by taking his wife to the Sassywood Man first. If he found his wife was lying, the husband would drop the charges and probably divorce her.

We arrived at court before the husband and wife and were rewarded with front row dirt seats outside the judge's hut. Jo and I had already asked Amani what the appropriate title for his father was and Amani had told us to call him Old Man, a term of respect. So we did. Old Man didn't speak English and we didn't speak Kpelle, but there was much smiling and finger snapping. We were delighted to meet him and he was equally delighted to meet his son's teachers.

After the greetings were complete, we got down to the important business of preparing for the trial. The first thing Old Man did was to ignite a roaring bonfire, just the thing for a hot afternoon. About this time the husband arrived without his wife.

"Where's your wife?" Old Man asked as Amani translated.

"She is being brought by her family," the husband replied.

"Being brought," it turned out, was a conservative description of the process. She was being dragged and appeared ready to bolt at the first opportunity, which she did. The woman was half gazelle; the greyhound I had owned as a child couldn't have caught her as she leapt off down the trail. For everyone involved, it looked like a clear case of guilt. But the trial was still going to be held. I asked Amani if it was being carried on for our benefit, but he explained that it was legitimate for the husband to sit in for the wife. After all, he was the one who had to be convinced.

Old Man disappeared into his hut and came out with a wicked-looking machete, a can of 'medicine' or magical objects, a pot of mystery liquid and a pot of water. He promptly shoved the machete's blade into the fire. Next, he dumped his can of magic objects on the ground. Included were two rolls of Sassywood leaves and several small stones of various colors and shapes.

Uh-oh, I thought to myself. Are we about to witness something here with the Sassywood leaves that we would just as soon not see?

But Old Man had a use for them other than ingestion. He asked the husband to sit down on the ground opposite him and place one roll of the leaves under his right foot. He placed the other roll under his own right foot. Both men wore shorts and had bare feet. It appeared we were to witness a trial by osmosis.

Next he studied where his magic objects had fallen on the ground and proceeded to mumble over them like a priest preparing for Communion. Once the appropriate spirits had been called, it was time for mystery liquid. A generous amount was rubbed on each Sassywood leg. We were ready for the truth.

"If the knife is cold, the woman is lying," Old Man declared dramatically as he pulled the glowing machete from the fire.

He took the "knife" and rubbed it down his leg. It sounded like a hot grill cozying up to a T-bone steak. But Old Man grinned. *The knife was cold.*

The husband was next. His leg appeared much less optimistic about the process. It was, in fact, preparing to follow his wife's legs lickety-split down the hill. A firm glare from Old Man made the leg behave. The machete sizzled its way down the shinbone and a look of surprise filled the husband's eyes. The knife was cold; the woman was lying.

We had to be absolutely sure, however, so Old Man shoved the machete back in the fire. This time he rubbed water up and down his and the husband's legs instead of mystery fluid. He then threw his magic rocks and commenced mumbling over them again. After about fifteen minutes he was ready for the final phase of the trial. He yanked the machete from the fire a second time.

"If the knife is hot, the woman is lying," he instructed as he reversed the directions.

"Ow!" he yelled and jumped back as the machete barely touched his leg! The knife was definitely, absolutely, beyond the shadow of a doubt, hot.

This time Old Man couldn't even get near the husband's leg since the husband had jumped up from his sitting position and was strategically located ten feet away. The jury had returned its verdict; his wife was lying and he would drop the charges. He didn't need his leg torched to prove the point.

All of these elements of tribal culture were fascinating to me. There were aspects of what the Kpelle believed, such as the spirit in the cottonwood tree, that I could almost believe myself. I like the pantheistic concept of spirits existing in plants, animals, and places as well as people. It implies an element of sacredness, interconnectivity and respect for the world around us that was lost ever so long ago when we decided that humankind was the hottest stuff in creation.

There also was a lot I didn't believe in but could recognize had value. The Lightning Man, Sassywood Man and the Bush Devil played important roles in maintaining order within the tribal society. They served as policeman, judge and priest.

Think of the power of the Lighting Man as a deterrent to crime. It's almost biblical. Given our scientific knowledge of how lightning works, it's easy to be amused by the concept of lightning striking bad guys. But is our system all that different? Our society requires almost as much faith to operate as the Kpelle's.

The use of Juju to make people become sick and die was totally lacking in value. It was both dark and dangerous. Left unchecked, such practices can and do lead to dire consequences. Some of the more macabre aspects of the violence that has haunted Africa over the past decades may be traced to this abuse of the 'dark arts.'

Speaking of dark, it is now time to report on how our home was invaded at night, again. Remember, the first invasion was soldiers. They wanted to pack me off to jail for Boy's crimes. This time the invaders wanted to eat our house.

CHAPTER 32

A LESSON ON EATING TERMITES

It's almost impossible to contemplate life in the jungle without thinking of bugs. Think of every jungle movie you have ever seen, every TV documentary you have watched, and every National Geographic article you have read; tropical rainforests are creepy, crawly places.

Leeches that suck your blood, ants that march in armies, and mosquitoes that ooze with malaria are all legendary representatives of jungle lore. Anyone who writes about the jungle is expected to include bug stories. So here are some bug tales.

I've already introduced you to bug-a-bugs, or termites as we more prosaically call them. If we listened very quietly in our first house, we could almost hear them dismantling the place around us, bite by bite. They were everywhere. The rainforest was full of their skyscrapers, huge mounds that have been known to reach forty feet into the air. An equivalent human building would be over nine miles high.

Americans are, of course, familiar with the voracious appetite of termites, but they may not be aware that termites in turn are considered to be tasty treats by a substantial portion of the animal kingdom.

Jo Ann and I learned this at the beginning of rainy season. This is when the little buggers sprout wings and fly in the millions to set up new colonies. We had a vague concept of what insect migration meant. We had seen ladybugs and other insects swarm when we were growing up. What we weren't prepared for was the sheer massiveness of the invasion.

Somewhere in the middle of night, we woke up with rain pounding against our shutters. At least we thought it was rain until we realized that it was only pounding on one shutter, the one protected by our porch roof. Curiosity led me to go exploring.

When I opened the door, the first thing I noticed was that we had left the porch light on. The second was that the sky was alive with flying termites, all of which seemed determined to land on the wall and shutters next to the light. Once landed, they immediately begin to move downward, making room for more bugs. I'm sure their greedy little minds were contemplating the wood beams that held up the porch.

Whether they could get to the beams was something else. Every animal in the neighborhood including Do Your Part, Brownie Girl, Puppy Doodle, and Rasputin were scarfing up bug-a-bugs as fast as their tongues and mouths could work. The ones they failed to gobble down were being eaten by a huge army of toads that ranged in size from teeny-tiny to humongous.

I called for Jo to come out and watch the carnage for a few minutes and then we retired back to bed, leaving the light on. We didn't have the heart to deprive the animals of their feast. The next morning I headed out to survey the damage. Not a termite was to be seen. It appeared that the animals and toads had hung around until the last bug-a-bug had disappeared off the platter. I was eager to get to school that morning so I could learn more about the termites' swarming habits from my students.

What I learned was that my students enjoyed eating the bug-a-bugs as much as the animals. Many of the students, in fact, showed up in class carrying cans loaded with the still-alive and squirming termites, which they proceeded to pop into their mouths for breakfast as we went through the day's first lesson.

"Sweet meat, Mr. Mekemson," they reported while making a smacking sound with their lips. "Would you like to try some?"

I primly informed them I preferred my food a little less rambunctious and without quite so many legs.

"The queens are best," one of the students stated authoritatively and was immediately backed up by a chorus of agreement. Queen termites are huge egg-laying machines with fist-sized abdomens capable of popping out 30,000 kiddos a day. The Liberians caught them by tearing apart the termite mounds. Appropriate eating etiquette involved biting off their tails and sucking out their innards. Sweet meat indeed!

Later that day I watched as Mr. Bonal's sister-in-law spread out mats for drying dead termites. The termites were then stored away for later feasting. Nothing edible was ever wasted in Liberia, whether it was flying meat, running meat, swimming meat or crawling meat.

And yes, we did get to try dried bug-a-bugs in Liberian chop. They were crunchy.

Third time's a charm, right. As noted, our first night invaders wanted to carry me off to jail, and the second wanted to eat our house. The third wanted to eat me.

CHAPTER 33

THE INVASION OF THE ARMY ANTS

Driver ants (better known as army ants) make great subjects for jungle-bug horror stories. There's a reason; these guys are ferocious.

I first experienced their ferocity when I was hiking through the jungle near Gbarnga and discovered a line of them crossing my path. At first glance, they looked like any other group of respectable ants negotiating a trail and minding their own business. On closer inspection, however, I found myself facing a tunnel of knife-sharp jaws, each one wide open and wanting to crunch down on something. Me. The larger soldiers had linked their hind legs and were facing out, creating a tunnel for the other ants to crawl through.

Always up for a challenge, I took a stick and poked the tunnel. Chomp! I yanked the stick back. The whole platoon of linked soldiers came along for the ride and a high-speed foot race commenced. I was both the finish line and first prize. Or at least I was supposed to be. I gave the ants a free flying lesson. It's possible they are still searching for their lost comrades.

Army ants are well known for their bite. In some parts of Africa they are reputedly used as sutures. Once their jaws clamp shut, they are locked. I can attest to this since one managed to get at me through a hole in my tennis shoe. They are also noted for eating anything that can't move fast enough to get out of their way. I watched as they gobbled down an unfortunate mouse. Their squeaking dinner simply disappeared under a sea of black.

Some villagers clear out of their huts when the ants come to town. The ants go through the huts, eat all of the bugs, mice, occasional snake and anything else alive, and then move on. It's a good deal for the villagers and the ants. My own attitude about our house being invaded wasn't nearly as positive.

It all started on a quiet tropical evening. I was reading a James Bond novel, Jo was preparing lesson plans, and Sam was glued to our phonograph, still trying to get Charlie off the MTA. I looked up and noticed a hoard of tiny insects frantically crawling under the screen door.

"Ants," Sam said

"No, Sam," I said, assuming my teacher role, "these are not ants." I was rewarded with an exasperated 'I know that' look from Sam.

"They are running away from ants that want to eat them," he jumped in to interrupt any further explanations on my part. He was right, as usual. I turned on the porch light. Anything that could hop, crawl, walk or run was seeking sanctuary in our house. Behind them came the ants. They weren't organized in a neat line this time. They were spread out across our yard and bearing down on us like a tsunami.

Jo and I held a hurried council of war. It was time to bring out the big gun, SHELLTOX. Shelltox was one of those marvelous nerve gasses created by the pesticide industry that was so potent it was banned in the US. The tiniest spurt of the poison would cause a cockroach to roll over and yell "uncle." We used it liberally.

Each of us picked up a can and stomped off to war. The stomping was serious; it kept the ants off. Back and forth along the enemy line we marched, spraying the ants and filling the air with whatever odor Shell incorporated into its brew to let us know we were poisoning ourselves. The ants died by the hundreds and soon by the thousands. But still they came on. Our cans begin to sputter. Exiting stage left was rapidly becoming our only alternative.

I pictured us packing up Rasputin and descending on the Peace Corps rep the way the ants had descended on us. First, we would tackle his liquor closet and then we would eat all of his food. Unfortunately, the ants blinked first. Their buglers blew retreat. We had won the battle, but the war was far from over.

That night, visions of monstrous ants visited me whenever I closed my eyes. Every hour we arose from bed to check if the attack had been renewed. Happily it hadn't. By morning, we had deluded ourselves into thinking that the ants had moved on to easier targets. But they had another plan. Mr. Bonal was wandering around outside his house so I went over to tell him our invasion story.

"Ah, let me show you something, Curtis," he said. He walked me over to an old pile of mud bricks buried in the grass twenty feet away from our front porch. I looked down. All I could see was a moving black mass! The area was carpeted with a layer of driver ants several inches thick. There were zillions of them.

"Welcome to the ants' home," John explained. "They have moved in for the rainy season."

The Bonals, it turned out, had been invaded the week before when Jo and I were in Monrovia. It had also been a night attack. The ants had crawled up the wall and through an open window into the baby's room. The baby, objecting strenuously to being a one-course meal, had started screaming, quite loudly. The family had come on the run. The baby was saved and the ants repulsed.

John assured me that the ants would be back to visit us again and again until they moved on. I decided to remove the welcome mat. But, first, Jo and I had to restock our ordinance supplies. Off we went to town for ump-teen cans of Shelltox, five gallons of kerosene, and a box of DDT. (Years later, after I became a certified greenie and read the book *Silent Spring*, I occasionally had twinges of guilt about the DDT.)

Our plan was to attack the home base with the kerosene, disorient the troops, destroy the barracks, and send the army packing. Of course there was a chance that the packing would be toward our house rather than away from it. In that case, our first line of defense would be to mount an all-out attack with Shelltox, as we had before. As a fallback position, I scratched a narrow ditch, i.e. *moat*, around our house and filled it with DDT. The ants would have to crawl through the stuff to get at us.

Then I went to work. Reaching the nest without becoming ant food was the first challenge. Having grown up in red-ant country, I remembered how sensitive ants are about their home territory. The slightest disturbance brings them boiling out of the ground in a blind rage. Apaches used the red ants' proverbial ferocity as a means of torturing enemies. I rightfully determined that the driver ants were meaner and faster than their distant cousins. They would be on me and up the inside of my pants leg in a flash, a fate to be avoided at all costs.

The initial strategy of removing vegetation was relatively safe. Sam and I stood several feet away and tossed two gallons of kerosene on the nest. A carefully cast match created a raging inferno that proved quite effective in defoliating the area.

Digging into the nest was much more dangerous; I would be operating behind enemy lines facing thousands of steel-jawed troops on a hunt-and-destroy mission. My solution was to draft a galvanized steel tub, which Jo and I had used for bathing at our first house. It provided ample standing room, and the ants couldn't crawl up the side. I tossed the tub next to the nest and leapt in. Sam tossed me our shovel. Several minutes of dedicated digging brought me to the mother of all nurseries. Eggs covered an area at least three feet across and several inches deep. Right in the middle was a finger sized, bright orange snake.

"Very poisonous," Sam said. I figured it had to be pure poison for the ants to leave it alone. We decided to take a break and let the ants and the snake work out their relationship.

After our standard lunch of a peanut butter and jelly sandwich washed down by orange Kool Aid, we went out to check the results of our handiwork. Success! Long lines of ants, many dragging eggs, stretched off into the distance *away* from our house. The siege was over. There was no sign of the snake, by the way. Maybe the ants had stopped for lunch as well.

CHAPTER 34

FROM FLYING RHINOS TO MINCING MAMBAS

Most of our bug encounters were less traumatic. Indeed, some, such as our interaction with rhinoceros beetles, we classified as entertainment.

These large bugs are a throwback to ancient times. In addition to being a good three inches long, they are coated with armor. The males have a huge horn projecting up from their noses; thus the name. They are reputedly the world's strongest animal and can carry up to 850 times their own weight. Liberian children would tie a thread around their horns and fly them in circles.

When we went outside after dark with a flashlight, they would dive-bomb the light and crash into us Kamikaze-style. It hurt. The buzzing noise made by their wings meant that we could hear them coming in time to flinch.

One very slow night when the minutes were ticking hours, I gathered several large males and one lone female on our cement porch. What ensued was an elaborate mating ritual: beetle foreplay. The one with the biggest horn got the girl. Their encounter had all of the grace of two Sherman tanks deciding to reproduce.

"Get a life, Curt," Jo Ann suggested.

Another insect of note was the sausage bug mentioned earlier as doggy treats. These insects were large flying abdomens. They would buzz in lazy circles through our house at night, flying so slowly that Jo and I used them for badminton practice, knocking them out of the air with our rackets. Afterwards, Do Your Part would be invited in to clean up the carnage. Based on her enthusiasm, they must have been quite tasty.

The best action by far was on the big screen— our screen door that is. Here we witnessed the law of the jungle in action. The bright lights of our house guaranteed that a hoard of small juicy insects would be attracted and clamor for admission. The opportunity for a free lunch quickly attracted a crowd of gourmet bug-eaters. It was the bug-a-bug feast all over except the players were different and less greedy. There was a lot more stalking and a lot less gobbling.

Knobby-toed iridescent tree frogs would suction-cup their way across the screen at a glacial pace and then unleash a lighting-fast tongue on some unsuspecting morsel. An eight-inch long praying mantis was a regular visitor until Jo Ann did it in, wrapped it up, and shipped it off to her old zoology instructor back at Sierra College. He reported to Jo that the monster never made it. I suspect someone in the Monrovia Post Office opened the box looking for treasure. Surprise!

My favorite predators were the bats. They would fly quick circles around the house and pick a bug off the screen with each circuit. I'd place my face a few inches from the screen to capture the night's activities. Whoosh, a bat would grab a bug for dinner. Zap, the pinkish white frog tongue would unfurl and reel in dessert. An evening at the movies was never better.

Another denizen of the rain forest that receives considerable press is the snake. As a youth, I had become aware of their treacherous ways by reading Tarzan comic books. The ape-man would throttle a 20-foot boa and then pound on his chest. We encountered a number of the wily serpents in our two years. They came in a myriad of sizes, shapes, and colors. I've already mentioned the tiny orange snake in the driver ants' nest. "Very poisonous," Sam had said.

I found a heart-stopping snake coiled around a sturdy stem in our flower garden when I was pulling weeds. Another time, his big brother times five posed in a tree above my classroom door. The whole school stopped by, but no one would walk into my classroom. One dark, rainy night Jo and I were walking home from chaperoning a high school dance. Our flashlight was on the verge of dying. I looked down and found my foot three inches away from a snake that stretched all the way across the road, which was just about the distance I managed to jump.

As I mentioned earlier, Liberians, including our cat, assumed that all snakes were poisonous. We decided while in Liberia to think as the Liberians did. The only good snake was one with its head chopped off.

The most poisonous was the cassava snake. This ugly pit viper is about as long as your arm and twice as thick. The snake is supposedly sluggish until you step on it. Then it whips around and strikes, causing instant death. On my jungle hikes I always encouraged the dogs to go first and watched them closely. Like Rasputin, they were snake-wise. If they detoured, I detoured— no questions asked.

We even had a giant boa constrictor hanging out in the neighborhood. It lived in the reservoir just down the hill from our house. Town folks would spot it occasionally slithering through the lake like the Loch Ness monster. I started calling it Nessie. Whenever a local dog or cat disappeared, it was assumed that the snake had eaten it. Responding to community concern, Soldiers eventually drained the lake in an unsuccessful attempt at finding the boa. Maybe it had developed a taste for guinea fowl and moved up to the superintendent's compound.

The green mamba was feared even more than the boa. This snake was said to climb trees, leap from limb to limb, and chase people. Jo Ann and I assumed that the Liberian who told us this story had been sipping too much fermented cane juice. At least we did until we looked out the window one day and saw a green mamba climbing our tree. Faster than I could say, "Let's sit this dance out," Jo had grabbed our machete and charged out the door. The mamba saw her coming and wisely made a prodigious leap for a higher limb. It missed. Down it came amidst a mad flurry of machete strokes. Not even the three musketeers could have withstood that attack. It was instant minced snake. After that I had more respect for Jo Ann when she was irritated.

In a slight reversal of roles, a snake did manage to 'tree' Jo once. I was happily ensconced in my favorite chair when I heard a scream from our outdoor bathroom. Talk about primitive male instincts. Hair on end, adrenaline pumping, and blood rushing, I grabbed the machete and sprinted to the rescue.

I threw open the bathroom door and there was Jo Ann, standing on the toilet with her pants down. Meanwhile a small black snake was merrily slithering around on the floor in hot pursuit of the little toads who considered our bathroom home. It had crawled under the door and across Jo's foot while she was sitting on the pot. Had it happened to me, I might have climbed up on the toilet, too.

Needless to say, I quickly dispatched the snake and saved the day.

CHAPTER 35

GOAT SOUP, GREED AND EVERYDAY LIFE

In some ways our everyday life as high school teachers resembled our everyday life as elementary school teachers. We would crawl out of bed at 6:30, eat a quick meal and walk to school. School ended at 1:00. Shortly after, we would be home downing peanut butter and jelly sandwiches. Our nap was next.

Our location encouraged wandering. We lived on the edge of town; the rainforest beckoned. After siesta, the dogs and I would disappear into the jungle. This continued a tradition of hiking in the woods that went back to my earliest childhood years. I explored the surrounding village trails going farther and farther afield. Sometimes I would take my compass so I could draw primitive maps and figure out where I had been. Tribal people were surprised to find me out in the bush but were always friendly.

I discovered where the cane fields and whiskey stills were, found a primitive but well-built wooden bridge across the river, made my first acquaintance with driver ants, and avoided numerous poison snakes.

Sometimes Jo Ann would join me. On occasion I would take Sam, other Volunteers and Peace Corps staff along. The hikes provided an opportunity to explore aspects of tribal life not normally found in Gbarnga. They also served as a major part of my exercise program. I became svelte, or maybe just skinny.

Our social life was nothing to write home about. Unlike single Peace Corps Volunteers, we had each other for amusement. We did maintain our friendship with other married Volunteers. Occasionally, students or teachers would drop by. Sam was always hanging around, even when not working. I maintained an ongoing chess game with the minister of the Presbyterian mission. We would send our houseboys back and forth with moves.

The largest social event we hosted was a goat feast for our fellow teachers from the high school and elementary school. Between finding a goat, having it slaughtered and making soup, it turned into a major project. Three women teachers from the elementary school came over to help with the cooking chores. They wanted to make sure the goat was properly cooked. The soup, poured over rice, was delicious, and plenteous. No one went home hungry, or sober for that matter. I'd bought two cases of Club Beer and one case of Guinness Stout to accompany dinner. Drunk driving was not an issue. No one owned a car.

Even with everyone stuffed, there was ample goat soup left over to feed the dogs for a week. It lasted a night. Liberian dogs always ate like they were on the edge of starvation, especially fat Liberian dogs. Somewhere in the midst of the four-legged feeding frenzy, I heard a yip and went outside to find that Brownie Girl had shoved a goat bone through her cheek. The medical emergency was minor; her real concern was being knocked out of the action. The other dogs and Rasputin were gobbling down her share. I pulled the bone out and Brownie Girl jumped back into the fray. It was pure greed. Not a scrap was left in the morning.

One of my favorite past times was to sit outside in the late afternoon, drink a gin and tonic, and watch the incredible tropical lightning storms. We found a jeep seat somewhere that made a comfortable couch for our porch. On occasion, the sky would turn an ominous black and we could hear the storm as it ripped through the rainforest. The impending mini-hurricane would send Jo and I scurrying to yank clothes off the clothesline and batten down the hatches– in other words, make sure doors and shutters were firmly closed.

Every month or so, we would visit Monrovia for a touch of city life. We even took Sam with us once for his 'birthday.' He really didn't know when his birthday was so we declared it took place during the trip. He still uses the same date.

Eating at a French restaurant in Monrovia by candlelight, shopping for an hour in an air-conditioned supermarket, perusing the shelves of a bookstore, visiting with friends, and seeing a movie did wonders for our morale. Our biggest break from life in Gbarnga and teaching, however, was a one-month trip to the big-game parks of East Africa.

CHAPTER 36

AFRICAN SAFARI BY VW BUG

African water buffalo are known for their nasty attitudes, and we were facing a whole herd of nastiness. Thirty minutes earlier, the gas pedal linkage on our Volkswagen Beetle had broken on our trip through Manyara National Park in Tanzania. We had jury-rigged a temporary fix by tying the pedal down. Stopping involved pushing the clutch in while the engine revved at full throttle. It was loud.

The herd of water buffalo crossing the road in front of us apparently didn't like loud. Or maybe it was just my imagination. I get nervous when 2000-pound beasts with large, formidable horns are contemplating a charge. The fact that our VW Bug tipped the scales at just over 1700-pounds and all its horn could accomplish was a puny beep, did not reduce my anxiety.

My travel companions, Jo Ann, John and Chris, were already nervous. Earlier in our exploration of the park, I had received a solid lecture for stopping and getting out to snap pictures of an elephant family. The week before a bull elephant in Manyara had caught a whiff of tourists in a VW Van and chased them down the road in an earth-pounding run. When he caught up, the seven-ton giant had rammed his tusks through the rear window.

Fortunately, neither the elephants nor the water buffalo considered our tiny car and its inhabitants worthy opponents. Just after dark we drove the limping VW back into our lodge overlooking the Rift Valley and Manyara National Park. We had successfully accomplished another adventure in our 2500-mile safari through East Africa.

Peace Corps Volunteers in Liberia were encouraged to go on vacation during the second January school break of their two-year tour. The majority of Group VI had chosen to charter a jet to East Africa for our month of escape. Our share of the charter had seriously depleted Jo Ann's and my savings, thus the self-guided VW safari. We hooked up with another married couple, John and Chris Ogden from New York, to share the adventure. Like Jo and me, John and Chris had graduated from college in 1965, married and joined the Peace Corps.

The airplane landed in Nairobi, Kenya– an attractive, modern city where we could actually drink the milk. It is amazing how much meaning such a small thing can assume. I would have been happy to just hang out and enjoy the amenities, but adventure called; there were lions and gazelles and rhinos, "oh my!" We rented our VW bug and crammed in. Tsavo National Park with its narrow dirt road was our first objective. Our eyes were glued to the windows, searching for wildlife.

"There's an elephant!" Chris shouted and we screeched to a halt. It looked impressively big from the perspective of our VW Beetle. So were its droppings. We drove around rather than through them. High-centering on elephant dung was not part of the adventure. We spotted an ostrich and then a giant porcupine. John and I jumped out of the car to check out the big fellow. He stood at least three feet tall, had six-inch quills, and exuded a 'don't mess with me' attitude. We called him Sir. Just as dusk arrived we spotted our first zebras. John raced down the road to keep pace with them while Jo Ann and Chris squealed about juvenile male behavior.

Mysterious Malindi on the Indian Ocean came next. Visiting was like stepping into the middle of an *Arabian Nights' Tale*. Vasco da Gama dropped-anchor off the coast at the close of the Fifteenth Century and picked up a local pilot to guide him onward to India. He left behind a stone cross that still stands. But long before Europe came crawling out of the Dark Ages and Vasco da Gama began his perilous journey, Malindi had been an important port on the busy Indian Ocean trade routes. Goods from as far away as China had made their way through Malindi's bustling markets, and the words of the Prophet Muhammad had echoed through its streets.

We camped out on the beach in huts and were introduced to sailing by John and Chris. We also tried snorkeling. A native outrigger canoe, complete with three natives, carried us out to a beautiful coral garden. A jellyfish seriously stung me for my efforts, while Chris and Jo Ann received exotic shells from the natives for theirs. Unfortunately, the shells were still occupied by their rightful owners. After several days of hot tropical sun, opening the trunk of the VW became an exercise in courage. We ended up paying five dollars to have the shells cleaned. It was a small fortune for the guy that did it, but we thought it was a great bargain.

Mombasa was next on our agenda. We drove into town under giant, sculpted elephant tusks, a reminder of the role that the ivory trade played in East Africa's history. There was also a reminder of when tiny Portugal had been a major world power; dark, foreboding Fort Jesus looked out to sea with the objective of protecting precious spice routes to the Indies. What impressed us most, though, were the woodcarvings the city was famous for. Out came our wallets as we shipped off piece after piece to the U.S.

As we crossed from Kenya into Tanzania, Mt. Kilimanjaro slipped by, hidden in the clouds. Several volunteers from our group had chosen to climb the mountain. We opted for a more sedate experience and drove up its side to check out the coffee plantations. Heading on to Arusha, we dined at a hotel that Hemingway had frequented during his East Africa sojourns. Much to the amusement of my companions, a large swarm of flies chose to buzz around my head during dinner. Even more annoying was the Tanzanian waiter who chose to point out with a very British accent that I was using the wrong knife on my fish.

"That, sir, is your butter knife!" he announced in a booming voice. Hemingway would have challenged him to a duel.

I did have one important responsibility in Arusha: buying meerschaum pipes for Morris Carpenter, who had already returned to America.

Unfortunately, I kept one when we returned to Gbarnga and made the mistake of trying it out while enjoying my porch. It would be years before I could break the addiction. Tobacco turned out to be much more dangerous than the elephants and water buffalo we encountered at Manyara National Park.

Two of Tanzania's parks, Ngorongoro Crater and the Serengeti Plains, provided our best wildlife viewing in East Africa. Ngorongoro is an extinct volcanic crater packed to the rim, so to speak, with wild animals. We arrived in late afternoon and chose a nearby tent camp as home. There was a beautiful old colonial hotel overlooking the crater, but its cost exceeded our budget by a factor of ten. We consoled ourselves by going there to drink beer on its verandah and watch the sun set over the crater. The hotel's high-paying guests missed the experience we had that night of animals grunting, growling and grazing outside our bedrooms.

Mere mortals aren't allowed to drive into the crater. For that we needed a bona fide Land Rover and licensed guide. We paid the price and descended the thousand feet to the floor of the crater. Our first sight was a standoff between buzzards and hyenas over the remains of a zebra. Next we saw the King of Beasts, lying on his back with all four feet up in the air. Nice kitty. I felt a strange compulsion to rub his belly but resisted the urge. An ostrich performed a ballet for some reason, whirling in tight circles before dashing off on an important errand.

Ungainly hartebeests and wildebeests also appeared to have appointments and joined up in organized lines for their journey. A rhino, called George by our driver, just stood and stared until I was precariously perched on top of the Land Rover snapping his picture. Then he charged. The driver took off and I almost didn't, which could have gotten messy.

After Ngorongoro, we dropped into one of the cradles of humanity, a rather dry and rocky Eden known as Olduvai Gorge. It was here that the Leakeys discovered the skull of Zinjanthropus, a 1.7 million year old precursor to humankind. We were lucky to engage a guide who had been with Mary

Leakey when she found the skull eight years earlier in 1959. The guide took us to the discovery site and excitedly relived the experience. We were almost ready to grab shovels and begin hunting for our own ancient ancestors.

The Serengeti is so flat you can leave the road and drive across the plains. That provided an opening for all sorts of mischief such as chasing giraffes, ostriches and gazelles. We spotted a cheetah perched in a tree and drove under her. She didn't pounce. A momma warthog and four little pups, all with tails straight up in the air, provided a humorous diversion.

I discovered that tiny dik-diks, members of the antelope clan, are truly small. I was able to sneak up within two feet of one that was sleeping. Again we had the same feeling that we'd experienced numerous times during our journey: we were in the world's greatest zoo, but we were the ones behind bars. The animals ran free.

After the Serengeti, the majority of our wildlife viewing was over. Tended farms replaced wild bush. We drove around Lake Victoria via Kenya, crossed the equator going north, entered Uganda in its relatively peaceful days, visited Kampala, and made a beeline for the Victoria Nile, where we chugged up the river in a boat reminiscent of Humphrey Bogart's boat, the *African Queen*. Hippos dutifully wallowed in the mud, crocodiles slid down the banks, and Murchison Falls rumbled. We were at the point where the Nile River begins its long journey north.

Our journey, sadly, was coming to an end. We drove back to Nairobi, turned in our faithful VW, rejoined our fellow Peace Corps Volunteers, and flew back to Robert's Field, Liberia. Work was calling.

CHAPTER 34

TEACHER

I am not sure I earned the title of teacher at the elementary school, even though I put in the time and occupied the chair. I did learn that teaching was hard work, and I developed a life-long respect for elementary school teachers. I like to believe— had to believe— that I had some impact on the life of my students.

High school, though, was different. From the beginning I was teaching subjects I enjoyed: World History, World Geography, African History and African Geography. The best of my teachers in high school and college had brought these subjects to life and made them exciting and relevant. I was determined to do the same for my students. We debated, did projects and made maps.

As strange as it may seem, my high school African History course was a first for Liberia. We travelled back in time, starting with the exciting discoveries being made in East Africa about the early beginnings of humanity. We looked at the historic West African kingdoms such as the Songhai and Mali. We explored the impacts of slavery, colonialism, Islam and Christianity on Africa.

In geography we started locally and moved outward, from Gbarnga to Liberia to Africa and the world. Like their elementary school counterparts, my high school students found it almost impossible to accept that Liberia occupied such a small part of the African Continent. They became incensed with the idea, as if it were my fault.

I wisely opted out of teaching Liberian History. It's likely that I would have deviated from the Americo-Liberian version and been run out of the country. How could I teach the kids, for example, that Matilda Newport was someone they should idolize when her claim to fame was blasting their great-great-grandfathers with a cannon? Matilda, according to legend, had saved the tiny colony of Americo-Liberians in 1822 by firing her cannon into the mass of tribal Liberians charging up the hill in an effort to destroy the colony. Her success had enabled the Americo-Liberians to go on and dominate the country for the next 150 years, which was good news for Americo-Liberians, but not so good news for tribal people.

I even had to be careful what I taught my World and African History classes. The students were bright and would draw their own conclusions.

"Gee, Mr. Mekemson, the way the white minority in South Africa controls things is a lot like Americo-Liberians control things here."

"Oh really?" was about as far as I dared go in response. Things had a way of getting back to the authorities. Favors could be earned by reporting supposedly seditious comments to paranoid government officials, and I had already earned enough black marks from the second grade reader and Boy's appetite for guinea fowl.

But I didn't stay out of trouble. During our second semester at Gboveh, I decided that creating a student government would help our students prepare for the future. I argued that the best way to prepare for democracy was to practice it. Everyone, including students, teachers and Mr. Bonal, agreed. We pulled together interested students, developed by-laws, and set up elections. The students even decided they would organize and run for office on party tickets. Why not? It sounded like fun.

It never entered my mind that this relatively innocent gesture would strike terror in the hearts of Americo-Liberians. Once again, I had failed to comprehend just how paranoid the Liberian government was. Within 24 hours from the decision to create tickets, we had been accused by the superintendent of Bong County of setting up competing political parties to the Government's True Whig Party.

Student leaders were told to cease and desist or they would be arrested and thrown in jail. Mr. Bonal invited me over to his house and suggested I start packing my bags. There was no way that he was prepared to take responsibility. I didn't blame him. At a minimum he could lose his job, or he might end up rotting in a Liberian jail, or dead.

On one level, the government's paranoid behavior made sense. The True Whig Party was the vehicle through which the Americo-Liberians maintained control of the government and, more importantly, their privileged positions. The Kpelle Tribe was the largest tribe in Liberia and my students were becoming the elite of the tribe through education. A political party set up at high school might indeed morph into a national political party, given time.

So we eliminated the tickets and party names. We were then allowed to proceed, but I have no doubt we were closely monitored. I couldn't help but wonder which of my students or fellow faculty members reported regularly to the superintendent about my treasonous behavior.

Somewhat on the lighter side was the business of keeping the names of my students straight. It wasn't that I had a lot to remember; there were five students in the 12th grade, ten in the 11th and sixteen in the 10th. Most teachers would kill for that student-teacher ratio. The problem was that the students changed their names frequently.

John Kennedy was popular in Liberia at the time so there were several John Kennedys. Moses was also popular. Five trillion missionaries made sure of it. Kids would also take the name of whomever they were living with. Most of them had left villages and were trying to survive life in the big town. Adopting the names of the families taking care of them encouraged better care. Sam even told me he considered becoming Sam Mekemson, our African son. (That would have shocked the folks back home!) Finally, as students became more aware of their heritage, some switched back to their tribal names. What a unique thought that was.

All the switching made roll call a challenge. Students wouldn't answer if I didn't use their name of the moment. I finally adopted a rule that they could change their names but only at the beginning of a semester. It worked, sort of.

My school activities increased as time went on. I chaired the social studies department from the beginning. This wasn't too significant since I *was* the social studies department and my primary responsibility involved keeping me in line. (Some misguided people have claimed that is not an easy task.) I also took on more work for Mr. Bonal and eventually came close to functioning in the role of vice principal. Daniel Goe had returned to the U.S. for further education.

Jo created a high school chorus that became so good the county superintendent wanted her to create a Bong County Chorus. She gracefully declined. This was, after all, the same man who wanted to throw us in jail when Boy ate his guinea fowls, and was ready to kick us out of the country because I dared to develop a student government.

There were a multitude of other activities. I developed a library for the school by raiding departing Volunteers' book collections. For some reason I was roped into coaching the school's football (soccer) team, a task I quickly traded for volleyball. (There were four-year-olds in town who knew more about soccer than I did.)

I also created a local Boy Scout troop. I taught them how to tie knots and they took me for great jungle walks. Jo Ann contributed by sewing patrol flags. All in all, we kept busy carrying out the same type of work being done by thousands of Peace Corps Volunteers around the world.

CHAPTER 36

GOODBYE LIBERIA

When we returned from East Africa, a shift had taken place; Jo Ann and I had become grizzled, respected veterans. Peace Corps V had left the Country and Peace Corps VIII had arrived. With a year and a half under our belts, we were the folks to go to for sage advice. We were even entitled to reminisce about the old days. We were, after all, 24 years old.

My seniors took top honors in the national social studies test, competing against the best public and missionary high schools in the country. Apparently, I was doing something right; Cuttington College sent student teachers to learn from me.

Still, Jo Ann and I were surprised when Peace Corps requested we spend our last six months touring the country and working in different schools as master teachers. We quickly declined. Our skill level may have fooled Peace Corps, but it didn't fool us. Two months of teacher training and one and one-half years of classroom experience did not create master teachers. We thought it best to keep our little secret. We also had several projects going at the school, and we wanted to complete them.

Jo and I, along with other selected PCVs, were also asked to help develop a manual for future Volunteers coming into the country. I chaired the section on Liberian culture. According to staff, my experience in doing research for the second-grade reader qualified me for the task. I had my doubts but took the job seriously. I was fortunate to have several Volunteers working with me who came from different sections of the country and added depth about their regions and tribes.

Apparently our efforts caught the attention of the American Embassy in Monrovia. A State Department official was sent to interview me about my views on tribal culture and the future of Liberia. At least I hoped he was from the State Department–embassies also housed CIA agents and a careful line was drawn between the Peace Corps and the CIA. Our mission was based upon trust and that trust could be severely damaged if it was found we worked with the CIA. Whatever my visitor's affiliation, he came bearing a six-pack of Heineken. We talked way into the night drinking his Heineken and then doing serious damage to my supply of Club Beer.

But the future of Liberia was not in our hands. Jo and I had done what we could as Peace Corps Volunteers through our positions as teachers and our efforts in the community. We had gained tremendously from our experience in Gbarnga and hoped our students had as well.

Time flew, and the reality of going home could no longer be ignored. Our last days came and we said our goodbyes to friends, the school, our house and the countryside. We found a good Peace Corps Volunteer home for Rasputin and packed up our African treasures. Sam had already left to attend Liberia's top boarding school, and we were helping pay costs. A school assembly loaded us down with gifts and good wishes. It was sad to be leaving, but bearable. New adventures waited.

On the last morning, I arose early to go outside for to sip my final cup of coffee in Gbarnga. A doo-doo bird plaintively issued his comment on the world, "doo, doo, doo," and I found myself agreeing. The sun hit the rain forest and then the school. The first students were making their way up the hill. They waved.

Do Your Part came trotting over. Do Your Part who was my dog but wasn't. Do Your Part who followed me wherever I went. Do Your Part who had exquisite manners and never jumped up on me, jumped onto my lap and looked into my eyes. She was shivering; she knew I was leaving and her knowing made it real. It almost broke my heart. I said my final goodbye.

THE TRAGEDY OF LIBERIA

On April 22, 1980, thirteen Americo-Liberians were driven down to Monrovia's Barclay Beach in a VW van, tied to telephone poles, and shot without blindfolds. Rebel soldiers, acting under the direction of Samuel Doe, the leader of Liberia's coup that had taken place two days earlier, carried out the executions. One soldier was so drunk he couldn't hit the man he had been assigned to kill. Afterwards, the bodies were stacked in a pile and sprayed with bullets before being rolled into a mass grave. The massacre marked the beginning of a tragedy that would see the death of over 200,000 Liberians.

The international press was invited to witness the event. The names of those executed were a who's who of Liberia's history. Their fathers, grandfathers and great grandfathers had ruled the country for period of time stretching back over 150 years.

The public executions were as savage as they were inexcusable. But they were also understandable, possibly even inevitable. Thirteen years earlier a representative from the US State Department had visited me at my home in Gbarnga. He wanted my perspective on the future of Liberia. We talked into the wee hours of the morning. His first request was that Sam, the young Kpelle man who worked for us, not be present.

Revolution of some kind, I had argued, was going to happen unless drastic changes were made in how Americo-Liberians ruled Liberia. Five percent of the population owned the majority of the nation's wealth and controlled 100% of the political power. Tribal Liberians were widely exploited and treated as second-class citizens– or worse. Deep resentment was building; a time bomb was ticking. It would explode unless Americo-Liberians were willing to share economic and political power.

I was not optimistic. I related my experiences to the State Department official about setting up a student government at Gboveh High School and about writing a Liberian second grade reader. My goals had been moderate. I wanted my high school students to learn about democracy and my elementary students to increase their reading skills. I certainly was not involved in revolutionary activity. I was merely doing what Peace Corps Volunteers had been brought into the country to do: help educate and train Liberians for the future.

I suggested that the drastic reaction of Americo-Liberians to my efforts reflected the deep paranoia that existed within the ruling class. The second-grade reader featured African folktales and stories about tribal children pursuing such common activities as playing soccer. Someone in the government had decided the book would inflame tribal passions. Even though Peace Corps had received initial approval from the Department of Education and arranged for an editor, a curriculum specialist and a graphic artist to work with me, I was told by Peace Corps staff to abandon the project and never talk about it.

The Americo-Liberians' response to the student government was even more dramatic. My students had decided it would be fun to create two parties to run against each other, like the Republicans and Democrats. Seemingly, this was a direct challenge to the Liberia's single-party system, the foundation of Americo-Liberian power. Word came down from Monrovia that my students were to be arrested and I was to be run out of the country unless the make-believe political parties were eliminated immediately.

Americo-Liberians were not stupid, far from it. Many were highly educated and had attended some of the best universities in the world. They knew they were sitting on a powder keg. Change was coming and they could choose to embrace that change and help guide it, or they could resist and fight against it. They chose the latter course. They had controlled the tribal population since the inception of the country and believed they could continue to. People who challenged this assumption, even Americo-Liberians who believed that change was needed, were shut down, sometimes violently. Any change would be gradual, even glacial, and would have to support continuing Americo-Liberian domination. It was a recipe for disaster.

Tribalism was another issue the State Department representative and I discussed on that night long ago in July of 1967 as rain pounded down on our zinc roof, lightning lit up the sky and thunder rolled across the jungle. This was a challenge that all of sub-Saharan Africa faced. Primary loyalty was to the tribe rather than the nation and tribal lands frequently crossed national boundaries. I had understood the issue academically at Berkeley; I came to understand it personally in Liberia. One particular instance had illustrated the depth of tribal feelings vividly.

Jo and I were walking home from Massaquoi Elementary School at the beginning of our two-year stint when we came across one of our students lying on the ground, obviously very sick. His classmates were simply walking around him, like he wasn't there. Jo Ann was furious.

"Why aren't you stopping to help?" she demanded.

"He's not Kpelle," was the answer. It was a matter-of-fact type statement. He was from another tribe. The fact that he was a fellow Liberian and member of the human race didn't seem to matter. It is extremely hard to build a nation when such beliefs predominate.

The problem was not insurmountable. I felt my high school students had moved beyond the deeper currents of tribalism. They were proud to be Liberians. Tribal differences were noted with a sense of humor rather than passion. Education, it seemed, could overcome the negative aspects of tribalism. Americo-Liberians, to their credit, were working to achieve this objective.

I expressed one final concern with the State Department official; actually, it was more of a nagging worry. The dark side of juju, or tribal sorcery, lurked beneath the surface in Liberia. Newspapers occasionally included stories about people who had been killed and cut up for their body parts, which were then used in rituals to increase the power of the killer. People were also made sick, or poisoned using juju. Kept in check, such practices have minimal impact on society. But what if the normal laws and customs of traditional and modern society broke down? Would the use of 'magic' become more prevalent? And what would be the results?

I often thought back on the conversation we had that night as I watched Liberia descend into chaos over the next 25 years.

In 1971, four years after I left Liberia, William Shadrach Tubman, President of the country since 1944, died in a London Hospital. His Vice President, William Tolbert, assumed the reigns of power. Tubman had been a master politician with strong connections to both the America-Liberians and tribal leadership. Tolbert lacked Tubman's charisma and leadership abilities.

He did, however, move forward with Tubman's unification program. Some of the more odious America-Liberian customs, such as the celebration of Matilda Newport day, were downgraded or eliminated. The University of Liberia, which provided an opportunity for tribal youth to obtain a higher education, was upgraded. Roads were expanded throughout the tribal areas.

Tolbert also continued, and even expanded, Tubman's open door economic policy. Other nations, including Communist countries, were invited to invest in Liberia. It was a policy shift guaranteed to ruffle feathers in the United States. The US had long considered Liberia as its African beachhead in the fight against Communism.

In the end, Tolbert's efforts benefitted the America-Liberians much more than they did the tribal population. Extra money invested in the country ended up in the pockets of America-Liberians. Roads to the interior opened up vast new tracts of land for America-Liberian farms and pro-vided a way for the government to more effectively tax tribal people.

Among the America-Liberians, no one profited more from Tolbert's actions than his own family. Twenty-two of his relatives held high positions in the Liberian Government and/or on boards of major corporations doing busi-ness in Liberia. Wealth accumulated rapidly. The small Liberian commu-nity of Bensonville outside of Monrovia was renamed Bentol in honor of Tolbert and became a family enclave complete with mansion-lined streets, a private zoo and a private lake. The town's extreme wealth provided stark contrast to Monrovia's hopeless poverty.

In April of 1979, Tolbert made a fatal error. He arbitrarily increased the price of rice by 50%. Rice was the primary staple of the Liberian diet. The increase meant that urban Liberians would now be spending over one third of their average monthly income of $80 on rice. Students from the University of Liberia and other dissidents called for a major protest. Police ended up killing a number of the protesters and riots ensued. Tolbert restored order by bringing in troops from Guinea. He shut down the University, rounded up dissidents, and charged a number of them with treason. It was the beginning of the end for Tolbert, and for exclusive rule by America-Liberians.

At one a.m. on April 12, 1980– one year after the rice riots and ten days before the executions on the beach, Master Sergeant Samuel Doe, Liberia's highest ranked non-commissioned officer and a member of the Krahn Tribe, led a group of 16 soldiers into the Executive Mansion in a coup d'état, and assassinated Tolbert.

The majority of Liberians considered Doe's rise to power positive. For the first time, tribal Liberians, along with the more liberal, change-oriented America-Liberians, would have a chance at governing. While Doe's mil-itary-based, People's Redemption Council would rule temporarily, he promised a return to constitutional government. Open elections would be held by 1985. Doe also took an anti-communist stand and offered Liberia as a staging area for American troops if necessary. The US was pleased; aid to Liberia was doubled.

Ultimately, however, Doe was unwilling to relinquish power. He returned to using tactics that Americo-Liberians had relied on for decades. Freedom of speech and freedom of the press were curtailed. Dissidents and opposition leaders were thrown in jail on trumped up charges. Doe and his military junta began accumulating wealth. "Same taxi, new driver" became a common motto of the opposition by 1984. With the approach of the 1985 elections, Doe moved to solidify his power and emasculate or eliminate any challenges. When students and faculty at the University of Liberia protested, he sent in the troops. Open elections became a farce. Violence and intimidation became the rule. When elections were finally held in 1985, Doe had his own people count the ballots. Nobody was surprised that the final tally showed that he had won. The only surprise was that the percentage was only 50.9%.

The US, unfortunately, turned a blind eye toward the political corruption and intimidation. Ronald Reagan's Assistant Secretary of State, Chester Cocker, reflected the administration's position by declaring that the "election day went off very well… and was a rare achievement in Africa…" As was often the case during the Cold War, a leader's position on Communism was much more important than his or her position on democracy.

To make matters worse, Doe surrounded himself with members of his own Krahn ethnic group and stirred up a toxic brew of tribal animosities. An armed invasion of Monrovia and an assassination attempt by Thomas Quiwonkpa from Nimba County led to a brutal repression of the Mano and Gio ethnic groups by Doe's Krahn-led military. This, in turn, led to the next step of Liberia's descent into dark chaos.

The perpetrator, Charles Taylor, was locked up in an American jail at the beginning of 1985. By the time Taylor's reign of terror was over in Liberia in 2003, he would be the first sitting head of state since the Nuremberg trials to be charged with war crimes and crimes against humanity in an international court.

Charles Taylor's father was Americo-Liberian and his mother a member of the Gola ethnic group. Like many Liberians, he obtained his college education in America. After attending Bentley College in Massachusetts, he returned to Liberia where he served as Director of the General Services Agency under Doe until he was accused of embezzling nine hundred thousand dollars in 1983. He then fled to the US where he was subsequently arrested and held in a Massachusetts jail at the request of the Liberian government. He managed to escape in 1985, probably with outside help. He would later claim that the CIA enabled his escape. It's possible, but many Americo-Liberians living in exile initially supported Taylor and may have provided aid.

Taylor's escape led him to Libya where he received training and support under Muammar Gaddafi. By 1989 he was working out of the Cote d'Ivoire, organizing a military force from Mano and Gio ethnic groups who were eager for revenge on Doe. Taylor's objective was to exploit their anger to attack and overthrow the government. One of his former commanders struck first.

In 1990, Prince Y. Johnson, a commander of Taylor's from Nimba County, split off to pursue his own ambitions. Such disaffections of military commanders were to become common during Liberia's long civil war. These warlords, operating on a regional basis, controlled subsections of Liberia. Johnson's forces made it into Monrovia before Taylor. He seized Doe and then tortured him to death– an event that was captured on video and turned over to the press.

The twists and turns of what would happen between 1990 and 2003 are beyond the scope of this book, but what ensued was an almost constant, brutal civil war between various groups vying for power. The depth to which Liberia fell is best illustrated by the rise of General Butt Naked, Joshua Milton Blahyi. Blahyi earned his nickname in the early 1990s by going into battle wearing nothing but shoes. Being naked, he believed, provided protection against bullets. He also believed that sacrificing children and practicing cannibalism were important to his success. Many of his soldiers were young boys who fought drugged and naked, or wearing dresses. After he was "saved" and saw the light, Butt Naked claimed, "The Devil made me do it." Today he is an evangelical minister in Monrovia. You can find him on Facebook.

With Prince Johnson occupying Monrovia, Charles Taylor used Gbarnga for his headquarters. A peace, brokered by the United Nations in 1997, allowed him to run for President of Liberia, which he won in a landslide. One of his more popular slogans was, "He killed my ma, he killed my pa, but I'll vote for him." As President, he mounted a PR campaign in the US to reengineer his image. Among the stranger aspects of the campaign was providing the Baptist preacher, Pat Robertson, with gold mining rights in Liberia. Robertson went to bat for Taylor, but it wasn't enough.

Taylor's efforts at reengineering failed. Liberia was soon in the midst of another civil war. Taylor also became actively engaged in inciting unrest next door in Sierra Leone. It was his efforts outside of Liberia and participation in the blood diamond trade that eventually led to his being tried and convicted at The Hague. In 2003 he was forced to resign; in 2006 he was arrested. In 2012 he was found guilty of war crimes and crimes against humanity, which led to a 50-year prison sentence. Among the charges were terrorism, murder, rape, conscription of children, and enslavement.

Liberian women were critical to Taylor's downfall. Much of the credit goes to Leymah Gbowee. She provides a powerful example of what a committed individual can accomplish, even in the face of almost insurmountable odds. A deeply religious woman, Gbowee grew up and raised a family during the chaos of Liberia's two civil wars. Her work with child soldiers who had been deeply traumatized by their experience led her to become a peace activist with a strong belief that women needed to participate in efforts to end the violence in Liberia.

By 2002, Gbowee had become a recognized leader of the peace movement and had organized thousands of Christian and Muslim women to gather in Monrovia for nonviolent demonstrations to end the war. She even organized a sex strike: no peace, no sex.

Finally, on April 23, 2003, Taylor granted a hearing for the women. Gbowee served as the spokesperson. Her words: "We are tired of war. We are tired of running. We are tired of begging for bulgur wheat. We are tired of our children being raped. We are now taking this stand, to secure the future of our children. Because we believe, as custodians of society, tomorrow our children will ask us, "Mama, what was your role during the crisis?"

When peace talks began in Accra, Ghana two months later, Gbowee was there with a group of Liberian women to pressure the various factions into signing a peace agreement. Her message was even more direct: "Butchers and murderers of the Liberian people -- STOP!" On August 18, 2003, an agreement was finally signed between the warring factions.

2006 marked the election of Ellen Johnson Sirleaf as President of Liberia and, hopefully, the beginning of a new chapter for the war-torn country. Sirleaf has a long history of participating in and surviving Liberian politics that dates back to Tolbert's government. She has spent months in jail and years in exile for her political activities. While she initially supported Taylor as an alternative to Doe, she ran against him for President in 1997 and became a vocal opponent of his policies. She has a strong background in finance, has worked for the United Nations, and received a Nobel Peace Prize for her efforts to restore peace in Liberia. In 2011 she was reelected to a second term as President.

The challenge of rebuilding Liberia is monumental, however. The infrastructure of Monrovia and major communities throughout the country was left in ruins by the war. Today, ten years after Taylor was driven from power, less than ten percent of Monrovia's population has access to clean water and much of the city remains off the grid in terms of electricity.

Sewer systems, medical care facilities and roads suffer from a similarly low level of development.

Sam, the young Kpelle man who had worked for us in Gbarnga, eventually went on to become a physician (Dr. Kylkon Mawkwi). When he was employed at Phoebe Hospital after the war, electricity was available for only a few hours per day; clean water was limited; and medical drugs were either nonexistent or in extremely short supply. When he left the hospital in 2012, little had changed.

Huge numbers of unemployed people are a challenge to the stability of any government. Thousands of unemployed people live in Monrovia. Many are ex-soldiers. These soldiers have seen the worst that war has to offer.

Repatriating these men into becoming productive members of society and giving them hope that life can be better are herculean tasks. Lack of medical care and psychological support combined with unemployment is obviously not the answer. As it stands, these ex-soldiers provide a potential source of recruits for the next demagogue to rise out of Liberia's troubled waters. And some of the old demagogues are still around.

It frightens me to realize that the supposedly reformed but unpunished General Butt Naked roams freely in Monrovia. And I am concerned that Prince Y. Johnson is now a Senator from Nimba County while Jewel Taylor, the ex-wife of Charles Taylor, is a Senator from Bong County. While both redemption and reform may be possible for individuals, these people have a dark history. Are they truly committed to what is best for Liberia or are they driven by ambition and greed? Will they and their compatriots serve as forces to pull the nation together or drive it apart?

Corruption, a legacy from the days of America-Liberian government, continues to haunt the country. In a world where bribery is seen as a way of life, low-paid civil servants such as police officers see nothing wrong with supplementing their income by using their positions to demand bribes. Such actions undermine belief in government's ability to provide fair and just treatment. As the corruption climbs up the ladder to judges and other government officials, the potential damage is multiplied.

So what are the answers? Nothing simple, that's for sure. Change has to come from within. Liberians have to perceive and want a different future from what they presently have. They need to believe that such a future is possible, and they have to work together to achieve it. Leymah Gbowee provided an excellent role model. She proved that Liberians could work together in a common cause regardless of tribal background or religious affiliation.

Much of what outside governments and non-government organizations (NGOs) have done to help has had minimum impact. For example, relief efforts may be necessary to solve an immediate crisis, but do little to prevent the reoccurrence of the crisis. Even programs designed to address underlying issues will fail unless the people being helped take ownership. For this to happen, the recipients have to perceive a need for the program and participate in its development.

My friend, Kylkon Mawkwi, provided an example of what happens when recipients of programs aren't stakeholders. According to Dr. Mawkwi, an aid organization decided to build modern toilet facilities in a village where going to the bathroom meant walking out into the bush and squatting. A few months later the organization checked back in. The villagers were still heading out into the bush. The chief had decided that the best way to keep his shiny new restroom shiny and new was to lock the door. A lack of perceived need, combined with minimal community involvement in the design, development, and maintenance of the facility had doomed it to fail. An opportunity to improve the villagers' health by introducing modern sanitation had been lost.

Beyond a desire to change and a commitment to make change happen, Liberia's future depends upon maintaining peace and stability, reducing corruption, developing infrastructure, and providing opportunities for individuals and families to improve their lives. Success will require people from different tribes working together with the descendants of Americo-Liberians, and Christians working together beside Muslims. And it will require continuing support from outside.

Ever so slowly, progress is being made. The most important accomplishment of Ellen Johnson Sirleaf's presidency to date is that she has provided an era of relative peace and stability for the country. If future leaders can accomplish the same, the nation stands a chance to recover.

One measure of the nation's stability is that Peace Corps is now back in Liberia. The organization had exited the country in 1990 because of the danger to Volunteers created by the civil war. At the request of Ellen Sirleaf-Johnson, Peace Corps returned in 2008. Once again Volunteers are spreading throughout the country and joining with Liberian teachers in educating young people.

As I follow blogs of Volunteers presently serving in Liberia, I am struck by the similarities of challenges we faced in the 1960s, but I am struck even more by the differences. How could it be otherwise given the devastation the country has been through? We dealt with absenteeism, lack of supplies, corruption, and the daily challenges of living and functioning effectively in another culture. But our students and communities had never experienced the fear, psychotic behavior, and death the civil wars unleashed. Neither were we overly concerned with our own security, as Volunteers must be now. (Although I must confess that I was a wee bit concerned when the soldiers came pounding on my door with their guns at 4:00 a.m. one morning in 1966.)

Capacity building, helping people to help themselves, has always been a central goal of the Peace Corps. The Bosh Bosh project in Salala, Bong County provides an excellent example of what can happen when a talented and enthusiastic Peace Corps Volunteer is paired with a welcoming and supportive community. Charlene Espinoza from San Diego, California began her Peace Corps assignment in 2011. She has documented her experience on her blog.

Here's the short version of the Bosh Bosh story. The community of Salala built a house for Peace Corps Volunteers– even though none had been assigned to the town. Peace Corps was impressed. It posted Charlene, along with a roommate, Kristin Caspar, to teach junior high at the Martha Tubman Public School in Salala. The two were soon consumed with teaching, tutoring and building a library. A few months into their tour, they went on a brief vacation in Sierra Leone where Charlene came across a purse made out of brightly colored lappa scraps. (Lappa cloth is the fabric that West African women use as wrap-around dresses and that tailors turn into shirts and other clothing.)

Inspiration struck! What if she went back to Salala and introduced the concept there. Young women could be taught how to sew and develop marketable products. In addition to learning valuable skills, the girls would also be increasing their self-confidence. The Bosh Bosh Project was born. Bosh Bosh is a Liberian word for different types of fabrics.

Charlene, working closely with her Liberian counterpart at school, reestablished a local but dormant girl's club and recruited young women to sew lappa-scrap bags. The girls loved the work, and the project soon acquired several sewing machines. A tailor was hired to come in and teach the girls more sophisticated sewing techniques. New market lines such as purses and E-reader covers were introduced. Regular seminars in everything from women's rights to HIV Aids Awareness were also offered to the club members. As the products began to sell, profits were returned to the project, providing the girls with full scholarships to meet their education costs.

As the girls became successful, their self-perceptions begin to change. They now believe they have a future; they have hope. And they are eager to make a difference in their country. Most have a perspective similar to Comfort Thomas who is 20 years old and has a six-year-old child:

"I decided to join the Salala Girls Club because I liked the project's objective. I have learned a lot while being in the club. I have learned how to sew different things, and it has made me more aware of my own health through the workshops offered and has given me a better understanding of how to take care of myself and think about my future as well. When I graduate from high school, I want to attend the University of Liberia and major in Political Science so that I can work in the Ministry of Education, and help many indigent people in Liberia and around the world."

And this is just one story. Charlene's experience, with varying levels of success, is being repeated by Peace Corps Volunteers throughout Liberia. The work is not easy, far from it. Progress is often measured in inches, if at all. There can be deep frustration. But there is also progress: a radio station is started in Gbarnga, a student shines at a science fair in Kakata, 30 kids end up coloring on a porch in Grand Bassa. The impact goes beyond the obvious. Unlike most aid workers, volunteers live in the communities where they work, often without electricity, water, or other modern amenities. They bring a sense of friendship and stability into their communities. It is a powerful message.

Returned Peace Corps Volunteers from Liberia are also working to help the country, both collectively, as Friends of Liberia, and individually. Last fall, I received a call from Judy Reed of Madison, Wisconsin. Judy served in Liberia Group IV (1964-66) with my friend Morris Carpenter. In 2007 she and a friend, Jane Scharer, visited Liberia and reconnected with 15 of her former students who are now adults in their 50s and 60s. She describes the experience as "bittersweet." Many had barely survived the war years and most had lost family members to the conflict. Life continued to be hard. Their children had had few opportunities for education.

Judy and Jane returned to the US determined to help. They created a small non-profit organization called the Liberian Assistance Program and went to work. Former Peace Corps Volunteers, friends and community organizations jumped in and offered support. Today, as a result, a new school stands in the town of Cow Field with over 200 students and 15 employees. The principal is a former student of Judy's.

The organization, Friends of Liberia (FOL), was originally created as an alumni group for returned Peace Corps Volunteers in 1986. By 1989 the organization was centrally involved in raising awareness in the US about the plight of Liberians involved in the civil war, and in seeking solutions to end the horrendous conflict– a role it continued to play up until the close of the struggle in 2003.

Today FOL is focused on encouraging early childhood education, improving the skills of health care workers, and in fostering entrepreneurship. The latter involves helping identify, educate and provide startup capital to motivated Liberians who want to build small businesses. The ultimate goal of the entrepreneurship program is to support the development of a middle class, a move that is essential to the long-term stability and prosperity of the nation.

Peace Corps is only one of numerous private and government agencies offering aid to Liberia and other African nations. One of the most ambitious programs is being pursued by the Obama administration. Seven billion dollars will be spent on electrification projects in Sub-Sahara Africa. This program has the potential of making a significant difference in the lives of Africans, assuming it lives up to its promise of building internal capacity, balancing urban and rural needs, and using both traditional and renewable energy sources.

Liberia is blessed with natural resources. Used to benefit the nation, these resources can provide the base for rebuilding the country. Continued investment by outside corporations is critical. Obviously such investments require a stable government and a promise of profit, but they also need to be accompanied by decent salaries, training for the workforce, focus on local development, and protection of the environment. Balance between meeting the needs of the investors and meeting the needs of the country is critical.

The tragedy of Liberia is a tragedy shared by most other African nations. The past history of colonialism and outside exploitation combined with

Africa's own unique challenges such as tribalism, minimal education and lack of economic development, have left these nations easy prey to outside forces and internal abuse. From slavery, to ivory trade, to blood diamonds, to rare woods and even rarer minerals, Africa has been viewed as a way to instant, illicit wealth regardless of its cost in human life and suffering. It has also been viewed as a battleground between powerful, opposing forces. Colonial nations, various religious groups, and dominant political blocks have all seen Africa as a means to some outside objective. Even today, world powers eye each other warily as they invest in Africa's future.

My students at Gboveh High School in Gbarnga in the mid-1960s were as bright, caring, and ambitious as any group of young people. They were excited about their future. I have no doubt that today's youth share similar dreams. Given education and opportunity, they can become the backbone of a more prosperous, democratic nation.

Liberia is still very fragile and needs continued support from the United Nations, the European Union, the United States and other countries. What is needed, however, is independence, not dependence. The country, with help, has the potential of standing on its own and becoming a model for the rest of war torn Africa, not simply another tragedy in a long line of tragedies.

THE SCOURGE OF EBOLA

December 2014. As I wrapped up my book on Liberia last spring, the deadly Ebola virus slipped quietly across the border from Guinea.

In late June, a woman walked into Bong County's Phebe Hospital with flu-like symptoms. The symptons could have been caused by malaria or any one of several other tropical ailments. No one thought of Ebola. No cases had been seen at the hospital. By the end of the week, the woman had died of the disease. Within a short period of time, six nurses who had cared for her were also dead. The rest of the staff, and the other patients, fled the facility.

By late summer, Liberia was front-page news around the world— in a way it never had been during its 14 years of destructive civil war. A pandemic with the potential of killing millions had infected several thousand people, killing half of them. The future of Liberia that I had felt cautiously optimistic about, was once again skating on the edge of chaos. Neither Liberia's infrastructure nor its culture was prepared to deal with the devastation the disease was creating.

Peace Corps made the decision at the end of August to evacuate its Volunteers in Liberia, Sierra Leone and Guinea. Two Volunteers had been exposed to the disease and placed under quarantine (both are okay). Because Volunteers live and work in the communities they serve, the risk of further exposure was great.

Volunteers reacted with dismay. With short notice, in some cases one or two days, they were required to pack their bags and say goodbye to their friends and to the projects they had worked so hard to develop. Eugene Wickett, who worked in Gbarnga, captured the resulting heartache on his blog:

"The shock I feel, at the moment, is the sudden realization that my life has been inexorably changed forever. It is the helplessness that envelops you when circumstances so completely outside of your control tear down something you have poured all of yourself into constructing. And it is the grief and guilt of knowing that, within a few days' time, you will be leaving a nation's worth of friends, family, and loved ones to the mercies (and widely resounding effects, most importantly) of some strange and terrible disease."

The nature of the disease and the efforts to control it have been written about extensively. The media frequently updates reports on how many people have died and where the disease has spread. Missing from the story, however, are numerous secondary impacts. And these may be even more important than Ebola and the death it is causing.

Once again, Liberia's schools are closed and the education that is so critical to the future of the country has come to a standstill. Medical care, which was minimal to start with, is now focused on Ebola or has ceased to exist. This leaves other tropical diseases uncared for. Together, they have the potential of killing far more people than Ebola. Increasing food prices and food scarcity have added hunger as an issue. And finally, the crisis threatens the stability of the government. There is a danger that Liberia may fall back into the chaos it suffered during the civil wars.

Is there any positive news? I believe the answer is yes. For one, the world is much more aware of Ebola. The fact that this deadly virus has no respect for national boundaries has created concern on a worldwide basis. A massive effort is now underway to find a vaccine that will prevent the disease. Any future outbreaks can also expect quicker and more definitive action from international organizations such as the World Health Organization. Delay in response, this time, resulted in thousands of unnecessary deaths and the spread of the disease far beyond the village in Guinea where it began.

Efforts by the Liberian government, with strong international support, seem to be slowing the spread of the disease in Monrovia. New outbreaks in rural areas are being reported, however. The battle is far from over and may rage on for a considerable time in Liberia and surrounding West African nations. The repercussions will continue on afterward. Still, it is heartening that some progress is being made.

Finally, I believe, make that hope, that people in the United States and other developed nations are more aware of Liberia and Africa because of the crisis. Helping third world nations fight poverty, disease, hunger, illiteracy and internal strife is more than a humanitarian gesture; it is a matter of enlightened self-interest. In today's world, our fates are intertwined. Ebola has proven this.

I wrote this book because I wanted to share my experience as a Peace Corps Volunteer, including the rewards and challenges— plus some of the humorous things that happened along the way. But I also wanted to provide insight into Liberia, her history and her people. I added the epilogue on the civil wars and this postscript on Ebola to update what I had written.

I've decided to donate half of the profits from this book to Friends of Liberia (FOL). By buying this book, you too are contributing to the fight against Ebola and continuing efforts to improve the lives of the people in Liberia. They have suffered much, but continue to struggle on. They are worthy of our help. While many organizations are contributing to the fight against Ebola and need our support, my choice of FOL is based on three factors.

First, the organization is made up of individuals with concern and expertise on Liberia, including people who have served on missions in Liberia, experts on international development, Liberians, and Returned Peace Corps Volunteers. Many of FOL's members have devoted a portion of their lives to working in Liberia on community-based programs dating from the 1960s to the present. They bring a level of knowledge and empathy for the people of Liberia that few can match. Second, the organization is totally volunteer. Its only motive for existing is to help the people of Liberia. The majority of its funds, approximately 95%, go directly into supporting programs. And finally, while FOL is currently focused on the Ebola crisis, its long-term goal is "to positively affect Liberia by supporting education, social, economic and humanitarian programs." Friends of Liberia is in the business of helping Liberians to help themselves. And that is what Liberians want.

If you would like to learn more about Friends of Liberia or contribute directly to the organization including its efforts against Ebola, I suggest you check out its website at fol.org.

THANK YOU

First, thank you to each and every one of my readers. You make the effort of writing worthwhile.

Writing *The Bush Devil Ate Sam* proved both rewarding and challenging: rewarding because I was able to relive one of the seminal periods of my life, challenging because I had to stretch my neurons to the point of snapping. People ask, "How can you recall so many details from 50 years ago?" Fortunately, I worked for three years in Peace Corps recruitment and public relations when I returned from Liberia. I shared my stories with thousands of people who were eager to join the Peace Corps. The stories became etched into my brain.

As always, in a project such as this, several people deserve credit. First, not surprisingly, is my wife Peggy. Her support has been unflagging, and her sense of humor, legendary. I was, after all, writing in detail about my first wife. Even more to the point, Peggy's the one who had to respond to the inevitable questions from family and friends: "Isn't Curt done yet? Hasn't he been writing for years? How long can it take?"

The two people most likely to check on my progress, Peggy's sister Jane Hagedorn and her mom Helen Dallen, also deserve my gratitude. I met Jane shortly after I quit working for Peace Corps. She has been a close friend and strong supporter of my writing ever since. After vetting me for 20 years, she even introduced me to her sister. Helen adopted the book as a personal project. First she volunteered her talents as a retired high school

English teacher to review my first drafts and then insisted that she help pay whatever publishing costs were involved. As a mother-in-law, she gets a gold star.

Serendipity stepped in when we moved into our new home in Oregon. I discovered our neighbor, Margaret Perrow della Santina, taught courses in writing at the University of Southern Oregon. I was quick to ask if she would provide editing services. Luckily for me, she agreed. Her comments on content, editing skills, and words of encouragement have been critical to the completion of the book.

The list goes on. Morris Carpenter and I became friends at Sierra College in 1961. Morris, as it turned out, ended up in Liberia as a Peace Corps Volunteer the year before I did. We served together for a year and have remained close ever since. We had several late-night phone calls reminiscing over his experiences as a Volunteer.

Dr. Kylkon Mawkwi (or Sam Kollie as we first knew him) was born in a mud hut and went to work for us in Liberia at age 13. He would go on to become a physician. We've kept in touch through visits, phone calls and letters. I talked with him several times as I worked on the book. He has been an invaluable source of information.

Of course, I take full responsibility for what I have written. My views are my own and do not necessarily represent the Peace Corps or those who have helped in the creation of this book.

MEET THE AUTHOR

Curt was raised in the small foothill town of Diamond Springs, California. He grew up wandering through the woods and communing with nature. It was a great life. But he also learned a lot about transparency. Everybody knew everything about everybody else, which was more than he wanted to know. So he escaped the confines of his universe in the mid-60s and headed off to UC Berkeley where he learned that integration was good, war was bad, and that young people who held such views should be bashed on the head and thrown in jail.

He was waiting for his turn with the Oakland police while sitting on the floor of the UC administration building and singing protest songs with Joan Baez when he had an epiphany: he should make America a better place and leave the country; he would join the Peace Corps.

Berkeley and the Peace Corps ruined Curt for living the American Dream. "If you would only make babies, become a good Christian boy, and take up photography," his father had grumbled. Instead, Curt became an environmentalist and a health advocate, happily making war on polluters and the tobacco industry. For variety, he became a wilderness guide leading hundred mile backpack treks.

Every three to five years Curt quits whatever he is doing and goes on an extended break. Travelling through the South Pacific and Asia, backpacking throughout the western United States, and going on a six-month, 10,000-mile, solo bicycle trip around North America are among the highlights. This lifestyle came to a temporary halt when he climbed off his bike in Sacramento, met the lovely Peggy, and decided to get married— in about one minute. It took a while longer to persuade Peggy and her two teenage children.

Today Curt and Peggy live on five wooded acres in Southern Oregon where he pursues yet another career, this time in writing. Visit him at his blog: wandering-through-time-and-place.me. He'd love to hear from you. Or you can Email him at cvmekemson@gmail.com.